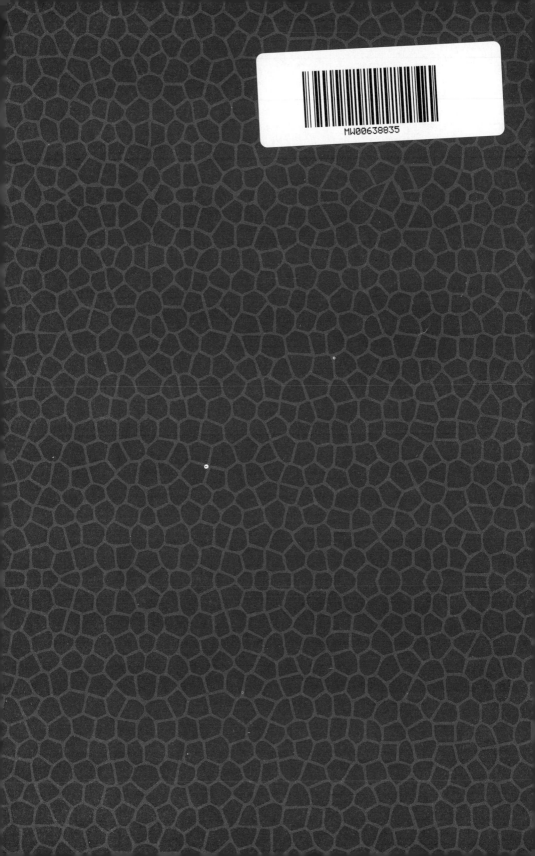

MOSAICA PRESS

# QUESTIONING THE ANSWERS

From the notebook of

## KAYLA HABER-GOLDSTEIN, FFB-BT

Published by Mosaica Press, Inc.
www.mosaicapress.com
info@mosaicapress.com

Chapter 1 is dedicated as a *zechus* for Jewish women
who are seeking their *zivugim*, as well as all the Jewish women
who are yearning to connect to their Creator.

ANONYMOUS

∽

Chapter 5 is dedicated for the *aliyah* of Malka bas Ella.

MIRIAM RUBIN

∽

In honor of Kayla, Shmuel, Shira, and Eitan
and their commitment to finding the *emes*.

With love and admiration,
NECHAMA, KOVI, HADASSAH, TOBA, AND ARYEH FLEISCHMANN

∽

In loving memory of Dovid Avraham ben Velvel,
my loving father who inspired me to constantly search for truth.

SARAH COHEN

∽

In honor of your dedication to learning and growing every day—
and helping others do the same. You are an inspiration to all
who know you.

MANYA LAZAROFF

∽

Dedicated by
SHANYA SHAFIER

∽

Dedicated by
LIZA KATZ

# ADVANCE PRAISE

One of the great *chassidim* of the Baal Hatanya was asked why he was so drawn to him. He replied, "The Rebbe is an eye doctor: he has taught me to see myself and the world in an entirely fresh and holy way." In Kayla Goldstein's marvelous book *Questioning the Answers*, the reader's eyes are opened to a clear, healthy Torah-true perspective on life and the fundamentals of our faith. Thank you, "Dr." Goldstein!

*Rav Moshe Weinberger*

Kayla writes intelligently and movingly about her journey to access *emunah* (faith). Her research led her to approaches that laid to rest both questions and answers that heretofore left her wanting. *Questioning the Answers* is well-written, user-friendly, and will unquestionably resonate with its readers. Thank you, Kayla.

*Rebbetzin Feige Twerski*

# TABLE OF CONTENTS

# ACKNOWLEDGMENTS

First of all, I really need to thank Hashem; without Him I obviously wouldn't be anything at all. But more than thanking Him just for existing, I thank Him for the support, love, and care I got from Him through this whole process. I really feel like He has my back, and I really, really am so grateful to have Hashem on my side. My new motto lately has been "I do my best, Hashem does the rest," and I cannot think of a better way to sum this relationship up. Thank You.

I also want to thank my husband. Shmuel has completely put up with everything I dream of, good and bad, and all my emotions; he is so, so supportive. He not only supports me emotionally but actually spends so much time helping me with my goals, dreaming with me, and planning with me. Shmuel sticks up for me and pushes me when I want to give up. It is incredible how he put aside his own feelings about religion and let me explore and find my own way, not worrying about how that would impact him. I could not have asked for a better partner, and I mean that. I am so grateful for him and where we are.

My parents are another gift from Hashem that I cannot possibly express my gratitude for. The love and acceptance I feel from them, the pride that they have in me, makes me so, so proud of what I am doing. My father has been there for me with all of my questions, has spent countless hours learning with me, and did not get upset or defensive even when I questioned his most basic beliefs. The way my mother is always there, telling me how proud she is and how I should be proud of myself and block out the noise, is so incredibly vital to being successful in life. The space I was given to grow into my own person is incredible, and I have my parents to thank for that. I thank them so much for continuing to be my support system.

I wish I could properly thank all the incredible people in my life, such as my siblings, my in-laws, and the amazing friends I have made along the way. Every single person who has supported me and loved me through this is more special to me than they know.

Not to be minimized, Mosaica Press, specifically Chana Harris, has worked so hard to make this manuscript complete, and I am very, very grateful.

And of course, my amazing, beautiful children, who are the reason I live and breathe. Shira Emunah and Eitan Simcha, you are my love and my life.

# Introduction

I'm finding it difficult to write this introduction. This book is not my personal memoir. However, it is important to understand where I am coming from.

Technically, the journey of this book began in 2016 when my son was born. However, in a deeper way, it began before that, as a young adult growing into myself.

I grew up in a religious home in Israel and went to schools deep in the chareidi system. My father is a well-respected rabbi and a very kind and wise man, someone whom I always strived to make proud. It is clear to me that this is why I never really rebelled—I didn't want to cause him pain. So I more or less followed the status quo and didn't get into too much trouble at school. Externally, at least, I kept up the life that was expected of me—by default.

I grew up, met my wonderful husband, and got married. We had a beautiful daughter and started our life together. I was very happy.

However, deep inside I had all types of questions—and doubts. I felt like the life I was living was…brainwashed. I had read a book about cults and vaguely felt like Judaism might be one. Deep down, some mitzvos bothered me, but I never did anything about it. I never even talked about it. Looking back, I think that I just didn't care enough to stop being religious, or to connect to God. It was easier to just keep doing what I had always done and what those around me were doing. I just moved through life, and "keeping religion" was just another (relatively minor) thing I did to keep the beautiful life I had created.

But these "minor" inconveniences started to get less minor when we decided to move to the States for my husband's job. Here, where I was no longer surrounded by the people I knew and loved, the positives for being religious began diminishing. The questions started coming up more often, and stronger. However, I still didn't do much about them.

Then, quite suddenly, my life fell apart.

My son's birth was incredibly difficult and almost ended tragically. I spent the months after in bed, unable to walk for more than a few minutes. I was overwhelmed. I was sick, mentally and physically—and I was angry at how hard things were. It was at this point in my life that I finally started asking questions. I was angry and hurt and I felt betrayed by God. Privately, I stopped being religious by default; I wasn't even thinking about it, I just could not be bothered anymore. I barely even wanted to live.

Life went on like this for about eight months. By this point, my husband was feeling a little lost. He supported me, wanted me to be okay, but he also wanted his children to be raised by someone who shared his value system. He needed a wife who would respect those values, and I wasn't sure I wanted to do that.

Around this time, my husband's rabbi was visiting the United States from Israel and kindly came for dinner. With my permission, my husband (Shmuel) told him the whole story and asked his advice. The rabbi looked at me calmly and asked me what my questions were. Here is where I hesitated. I knew what my questions were but, incredibly, I had never voiced them! Why? Fear of being yelled at or misunderstood, fear of disappointing or angering people, fear of hating myself…the list goes on. Whatever the reasons, the fact is that I had never, ever spoken them out loud. I refused to then as well, and I responded that I could not tell him what my questions were, as he would never understand and would call me an atheist. I firmly believe God put the next words into his mouth. He calmly responded, "Well, you know all Jews have questions. The smart ones find answers."

And so began the journey of this book.

I started asking questions. Hard questions. I had no agenda regarding what the answers would be. I wasn't looking for answers to fit a preconceived narrative. I wasn't looking for answers that would give me permission to do whatever I wanted. I was simply interested in learning about this religion—so I could decide if I wanted to be part of it.

Questions like:

- If God is so good, why do so many bad things happen?
- Why was I created?
- What about women's equality?

I asked about the tiny details and the big things, like the creation of the world and the reason we keep Shabbos. I asked basic questions too, like why we cover our knees, and why we have to wait six hours after meat to have a coffee, and I took notes of it all.

I started asking more and more questions, literally, all the time. Looking back, I'm proud of myself: I was asking sincerely. I wanted to understand why so many people were religious, and I was determined to find out their reasoning before dropping it all. I was prepared to give it one more real chance, with the sole focus of finding answers.

Sadly, however, answers were not so forthcoming. In general, in the ultra-Orthodox community there is a culture that frowns on asking these kinds of questions. The number of times I was told that we should have "simple faith" and "just believe" became too many to count. When I asked questions at tables at which I was a guest, I was told that "this is why women should not learn Torah." Even when I would go to classes to learn and I would ask questions, I was told, "It's complicated," or, "A good girl doesn't talk that way." It seemed like wherever I searched, I was being shut down. I began prefacing my questions with "I am asking to know. I really want to know." This helped somewhat, but I still wasn't getting real answers. I wasn't getting deep enough.

This experience was frustrating, to say the least. I was religious on the outside, empty on the inside—and had no one who could answer what I thought (really, what I *knew*) were legitimate and important questions. I couldn't go on like this, and I needed a solution.

After a few weeks of gathering courage, I called my father with a request. I'm still not sure why it took me so long to ask him.

I had created a plan and I called him, determined. I told him what I had been going through. And then I asked him why, if the Torah was really given to men, women, and children, it was so hard for me to get anyone to teach me about it.

I expressed how I felt as though Judaism were not really mine, that I was merely a servant in it. I let him know that I was on a mission to find answers. I asked if he would help me.

My father readily agreed. So, with my husband there for the day-to-day and my father there to give direction and answer the hard questions, they helped me learn, helped me learn how to learn, and helped me understand.

Incredibly, at the time I thought I was alone. I thought I was the only religious girl who was confused. Once I began asking questions more openly, I started sharing with my friends, and found many of them had questions as well. I opened an Instagram account and discovered even more young women like me with questions and doubts. Conversations developed and I realized I was far from alone in my confusion and doubts. So many young women, teenagers, and even older women have questions like me—and rarely find answers. Most don't even know how to formulate the questions. I became even more determined to answer the questions and write this book, to give women a safe space to explore, without anyone second-guessing their reason for asking. It is our Torah, and it should feel that way, for each and every Jewish man and woman.

The more I discovered, the more I was blown away by the answers. Things I never knew, things I was told to just believe in, were suddenly coming alive. I was on fire! I wanted to know more. Everything was making sense. My heritage was rich, amazing, and wonderful!

But suddenly I stopped in my tracks. I asked myself: Why did I have to wait more than twenty-five years to get these answers? If someone would have told me this when I was thirteen or twenty-one, it would have saved me so much stress and confusion. Yes, I could have asked, but I didn't know how to. I wanted to know why it was not taught this way to begin with. Why do some people never get these answers?

I now understand much better the reasons for so many seemingly arbitrary rules. I'm still learning—aren't we all, hopefully?—but I realized that once I was really open to listening, I was incredibly fortunate to have a father and a husband who were both qualified and willing to guide me and let me learn at my pace. The fact that my husband was okay with me exploring and doing things on my terms, in my way, was

incredible. I knew it was unique that I had the space to ask these questions and come back on my own terms. Not everyone is so fortunate.
I wanted to give this same opportunity to women everywhere. To teach
them why we do the things we do and to help give meaning to their
lives. To explain the thought process, the sources, and the ideas behind
our beliefs. This is our heritage!

It is hard for young women to ask questions without risking everything, especially once they are wives and mothers. I owe a huge debt of
gratitude to my husband for giving me that space and respecting me
through it. I am eternally grateful to my father for never once judging
me harshly.

Not everyone can ask and explore freely.

Therefore, this book.

Now a disclaimer: Before you begin reading this book, I would like
to point one thing out. There is a commandment in the Torah that
a judge is not allowed to accept a bribe. He is not even allowed to accept
a no-strings-attached gift from any of the parties in question.[1] This is
because it blinds him to the truth. No matter how objective the judge
tries to be, he can no longer be one hundred percent unbiased.

When it comes to understanding this book and any other book like it,
the same applies. If you are focused on your desire to live free of rules
and do whatever you want, then you will not be able to see the truth.
This book won't answer your questions because, right now, you aren't
really asking questions. I feel for you, but this book is not really for you.

But if you are looking for the truth and really want to know what to
believe in and how to live your life, this book *is* for you. As I mentioned
above, I asked these questions with no hidden agenda. I wanted to
know the truth, whether this was all real or not.

We ask questions to find answers, not to find excuses.

By virtue of you still reading this book after that disclaimer, I am
happy that you are here to learn. I am grateful that you are looking for
the reasons, meaning, and truth behind the rules.

---

1   *Shemos* 23:8.

Thank you for sharing in my thirst for knowledge and my curiosity about our heritage. Thank you for taking the time to read this book. What we are learning here is a long, unbroken line passed down generation to generation, starting with God. This is my heritage. This is my tradition. And it's yours, too.

It is your inheritance.

No matter what you have or have not done, no matter who you are or what you have been told, Torah belongs to you as much as it does to me or anyone else. Your relationship with God is unconditional. Take advantage of it. Own it. If you do not understand it, ask about it.

It is yours.

*If you have any questions, contact me at kaylahaber@gmail.com or find me on Instagram @questioningtheanswers.*

*Readers are encouraged to use the pages  provided at the back of the book for jotting down notes, ideas, and questions while reading the book.*

# CHAPTER 1

# THE CREATOR

Where do we start? From the beginning. Creation itself.

The father of thermodynamics, physicist Sadi Carnot, coined the phrase "You can't get something for nothing." This has been the basis of many scientific studies of the universe ever since. It is considered a foundational core belief of science today—and when you think about it, it is quite obvious, isn't it? There is no example anywhere in science, space, or world history of something coming from nothing.

So, we can safely assume that the world did not come from nothing; something was there before. Something created the world. It must have. It is impossible to have "just appeared." Some people think it was the Big Bang. For simplicity's sake, we are going to call it "the Creator" and not try to describe it. (Throughout the book, the Creator is interchanged with God.)

This brings us to our first question: How did the world come about?

Many other questions go hand in hand with this one, such as:

Does the Creator create things every day, or was it all created on the first day?

- Is the power of creation given to humans?
- Was the world created and abandoned, or is it tended to every second?
- Who is the Creator? Is He good or bad? A He or She?
- Does the Creator love me? Even know me?
- *Why* did the Creator create the world?
- *Why* did the Creator create me?
- And my favorite question: What am I supposed to do with all this information?

7

I know. It all seems overwhelming. Looking back, I kind of understand why I felt the way I did when I was growing up. These *are* big questions, and there are a lot of them. However, questions are nothing to be afraid of. When we have questions, we find answers.

Let's begin:

- Who created the world?
- Is the Creator male or female?
- Good or bad or in between?
- Terrifying or loving?

Before we delve into trying to understand the Creator, I want to share something my niece told me after she asked Rabbi Yitzchak Feigenbaum the following question. I think it is an amazing perspective.

She asked on behalf of a friend: If design implies a designer, who "designed" God?

Rabbi Feigenbaum responded:

> *My dear young lady,*
>
> *You asked a very intelligent—and very common—question. Your thinking is correct: If the world we see around us clearly demonstrates design, forethought, and planning, then there must be a Designer of Great Intelligence. But that begs the question: Where did that Designer get His intelligence? And the question could go on forever.*
>
> *There are a few responses to this. On the simplest level: Who cares? The only "Intelligent Designer" Who communicated anything to us humans is God Who spoke to three million of us at Mount Sinai and gave us a mission and His law (in which He Himself states that there is nothing before God). He also miraculously kept us alive for all these years, intact as a nation, front and center of world attention, even though we are less than 2 percent of the world population! So, it is an interesting question, and in 120 years, when you get to Heaven, you can ask Him, but it makes no practical difference to us now.*
>
> *On a deeper level, we are only humans. We can know what God*

*does and did, and we can know what He said, but as humans we can never know Who He is!*

*A hundred years ago, if you would show someone a piece of wood and they would ask you, "What is wood?" your answer would be, "It is something that you use to make chairs, and make fires." Now you did not answer "what" is wood, you told him what it does. Today we know what wood is, DNA and genomes (and we know what it does). When it comes to God, we do not know what He is. We are like a blind person speaking about a rainbow. We can rattle off the colors, but they are just words with no meaning that we believe do mean something because our friend who is not blind told us those words. Thus all we can know is that there is an Intelligent Designer out there, but we cannot know His essence. Thus to understand Who He really is, and thus His beginnings, that is beyond us.*

I absolutely loved this perspective. We can try and understand the Creator as fully as our human, finite mind can comprehend. But let's do so with the recognition that by definition—because we are people and He is God—our understanding will inevitably be limited. And truthfully, knowing "who God is" is less important than knowing what He does—that He is responsible for us, He communicates with us, and gives us to us, and what this means to us in practice.

So back to our list of questions, with a new perspective. Is the Creator male or female?

Surprisingly, in a way, the Creator is actually known to be both male and female. In his book *Inner Space*, Rabbi Aryeh Kaplan explains:

*While we cannot begin to imagine the Creator, as this is beyond the scope of our minds, the Creator did understand that the human being that He created needs to connect with Him/Her somehow. Therefore, in a basic sense, the Creator constricted Him/Herself into the Sefiros and used them as a bridge between the spiritual world and the physical world.*[1]

---

1    Chapter 1.

What exactly are the *Sefiros*?

In a simple explanation, they are described as emanations or attributes, and sometimes traits. What they are, in a long description, are the elements of the Creator with which He interacts with the world. Since the Creator is infinite and the world is finite, He wanted to create some kind of bridge connecting the two. For this, He created ten *Sefiros*, or emanations, through which He can be (partially) understood or described. It is through these ten *Sefiros* that the Creator interacts with the world and through which we connect to our Creator. Ten different parts of Him are revealed, out of infinitely more that we cannot understand.

Some *Sefiros* are masculine and some are feminine, implying that the Creator can manifest as both or as something else entirely. For the sake of simplicity, we refer to the Creator as "He." However, if you are more comfortable saying "She," you certainly can. As the *Rambam* says: "The Creator…is not physical and is not affected by physical phenomena."[2] So either way we are not actually describing the Creator; we are merely relating to Him in different ways to help us connect.

With regard to whether the Creator is good or bad, we can find an answer in *Tehillim*, the psalms written by King David. He writes: "God is good to all, His love rests on all His creations."[3] If King David thought the Creator was good, we can trust his judgment. Why is that?

King David did not have an easy life. He was born around three thousand years ago (circa 1000 BCE) to a farmer and shepherd in Beis Lechem. He was the youngest, with plenty of older brothers, and was considered the runt of his family. Though scorned, he offered to fight against the giant Goliath with nothing but a slingshot. Incredibly, he won. When the prophet Shmuel told him he'd be the next king, the sitting king, Shaul, was not happy—to say the least. Therefore, David spent many years in hiding so as not to be killed. On more than one occasion, he had to pretend to be mentally unstable to save his own life! When he finally did become king, his troubles were far from over. He fought many great wars and went through many personal tragedies.

---

2    Commentary to the Mishnah, *Sanhedrin*, chap. 10.
3    *Tehillim* 145:9.

(In short, whatever you are going through, however terrible and hard it might be, David could probably relate. Read the Books of *Shmuel* and *Melachim* to find out more.) Even in the book of *Tehillim* itself, written by David, we can see clearly the troubles he went through. So why would he have any reason to say that the Creator was good?

There are many explanations. The one I relate to most goes like this: We can know for certain the Creator is a giver. That is evident in the fact that He created the world; when you create something, you are giving to it—whether it is your talent, your time, or your belongings. Even more so when we co-create a human, we give it nutrients and space from our body. In creating, the Creator is a giver.

In order to be a giver, one needs a receiver, otherwise one is inherently not a giver. They can have the intent to give and the item to give. But without the receiver, they are not a giver. A gift is meaningless if there is no one to receive it. A teacher without students is, at most, a potential teacher—but not a real teacher.

Therefore, the Creator created humans in order to bestow on us all that He had to give. However, the humans needed a place to live, for a finite being cannot survive in infinite spirituality. So, the Creator created the world and everything in it—for Man, in order to give to us. He had no ulterior motive other than to give to us. We literally were created, with everything that was created with us, so that we can receive gifts! His initial will was all good, and everything that followed was and is all good. Think about it: Since He had no negative agenda, there was no negativity in the ensuing acts. From this we can deduce that the Creator Himself is good, for there is no evil intent in Him at all. Even if we say we may have angered Him so much that His intent became negative, we will see below why this is inaccurate.

In human terms, if one has the will to do something positive for someone else, not looking to get anything in return, he or she is considered selfless. Even more when it is an infinite being like the Creator. He did not need us, nor did He need to give to us. He wanted to for the simple reason of wanting to bestow goodness on someone or something. His intent was pure and contained no evil. From this, it is clear that there is no evil in any of Creation.

The Creator, therefore, is good. (Phew!)

King David understood this and therefore praised the Creator as good. However, a question arises, the same question we asked when it came to King David's life. If the Creator is good, the intent is good, and therefore all the action is good, how then is there evil in His Creation?

To answer this, we need to understand what evil is. Evil is not a stand-alone attribute. Rather, evil is the absence of good, much as darkness is the absence of light. It is there when good is hidden or taken away.

Why is good "taken away" or hidden? If the Creator's goal was all good, as we have seen, why would He remove the good in His Creation?

Let's go back to Rabbi Aryeh Kaplan's book to try to understand this: "The Creator wanted us to choose good so that we can receive good."[4]

But this sentence only brings on more questions. For example: Why can't we just receive good without earning it first?

Have you ever experienced closeness with the Creator? A moment of clarity and knowing? That is the best thing, the ultimate good. But how do we get close to something so unlike us? It seems unattainable. Usually when we are close to another human, it is because we share something in common, such as a struggle, personality trait, or value system. It is very difficult to connect to another human with whom we have absolutely nothing in common—all the more so with a being that is not even human. So how can we possibly connect to the Creator, who is so different from us, our minds cannot fully comprehend Him?

We connect to others by creating common ground. We create or discover a shared value or idea. With our Creator, we can do this by emulating Him. The *Tomer Devorah* teaches that emulating the Creator, and the resulting connection formed, is the ultimate pleasure and goodness in this world.[5] Since the Creator is all good, when we choose good, thereby making us "good" (even if it's just for that moment!), we are resembling the Creator and therefore have a common trait. In doing so, we reach the ultimate good, which is closeness with our Creator. That connection

---

4    *Inner Space*, p. 14.
5    *Tomer Devorah* 1:1.

opens pathways for more goodness to come to us from the Ultimate Giver. Amazing!

The Creator made it *our* choice to select good so that we can choose good of our own free will. In this way, we resemble the Creator and thereby enjoy the ultimate good of closeness to Him. However, to give us choice, there had to be an alternative option; as such, the space was created for evil in the Creation.

There is more to this, though. It goes deeper. God wanted to be a giver, and for this He needed a receiver. God had already created angels, so why did He create humans and a whole world to sustain them? Why not just give to the angels?

The Gemara tells us that when the Creator created the world, He created a group of angels. When He asked the angels what they think of the human, they asked the Creator, "What do You need them for? It is better not to create the human." The Creator then destroyed the angels. This happened with a second group of angels as well. Then the third group of angels replied, "It is Your world, do as You wish," and the Creator created the human.[6]

When the generation of Noach and the Flood came along, and later the generation of the Tower of Bavel, these same angels asked the Creator, "Why do you keep them around?" The Creator answered them, regarding humanity, "Even until they are old with gray hair, I will be patient."

This is astounding—and a bit confusing. If the Creator wanted to create a receiver with the intention of that receiver choosing good, why did He create them so flawed that they were capable of building a tower to fight Him?

The angels do not have freedom of choice; they are more "robotic." They do what they are commanded, without thought processes and emotions. The human was created and is the only other being that has free will, other than the Creator. In giving us the option to choose what we want, God also gave us the option to choose wrong—even to rebel against our own Creator. Again, why create us like this?

---

6    *Sanhedrin* 38b.

Rabbi Jonathan Sacks answers this in his class on *Parashas Bereishis*:

> *The Creator created man and sustains man even as he sins and rebels, because the Creator has faith in man. As mentioned above, "Until they are old and grey I shall be patient." It can take ten generations to produce a Noach, and ten more generations to produce an Avraham. For the Creator, it doesn't matter how long it takes. He created humans because He has faith that eventually we will choose good, and in doing so we will be the ultimate receivers, just as He is the ultimate giver. Yes, we could have been created with less free will, more of a moral compass, and have an easier time choosing good. However, then we would not have been the ultimate receivers. We would have been partial, mediocre receivers. With the ability to completely choose for ourselves, we are in effect becoming the ultimate receivers, and therefore the Creator can be the ultimate Giver.*

How empowering is that? To know that the Creator has faith in us, that no matter what we do, or how long it takes, He is patiently waiting, full of faith that we will choose the right path. He is sure He will be able to give all the goodness in the world to us, and is excited for when it happens.

There are "bad" things in the world. From our point of view, it ain't all roses and ice cream. Life isn't always easy. I've experienced it—and so have you. That is the point. He could have made us angels living on clouds. But He didn't. We aren't robotic and things aren't always easy or clear. He wants us to find the good, to choose to create the good, to try and be "like Him." That way we can receive from Him in the ultimate way.

Once we learn and internalize this, we can really start to grasp the meaning of Creation, the Creator, and what we are here to do. We can start, on a surface level, to see the workings behind the world we see and experience every day.

But this raises another question: How does the world function every day? What exactly is happening on a day-to-day basis? Yes, we understand initial Creation and the intent behind it, but does the Creator create things every day or was it all created in the beginning? How do my choices fit with His Creation?

One could say—and have a fair amount of proof to back it up—that the Creator created the world and then created systems and processes. It would be a reasonable assumption to maintain that the Creator allows the world to run on "automatic" after the initial act of Creation—like setting up systems, pushing the "on" button, and then leaving. Which, at first glance, would make sense.

However, if that were true, then how could the unnatural things that happen all the time be explained? Birth, miraculous recoveries, or even natural elements that need constant renewal? While many things are natural and seemingly logical, not *everything* is. If we open our eyes and look around, we see daily occurrences that aren't natural at all! We just have to be open to seeing them. The fact that a baby knows how to swallow instinctively, birds know where to fly, and huge trees come out of tiny seeds is kind of thought-provoking, no? These things are not normal, but we are so used to them, we perceive them to be.

What if all these happenings could be explained with science, i.e., nature, and you are not impressed? People sometime experience a personal miracle up close that leaves them with the knowledge that the Creator is involved and cares. But most of what we witness and experience can be explained by science.

This is a concept I struggled with for a long time. Pretty quickly, I connected to the idea that something can't come from nothing and that God created the world. However, for a long time it seemed to me that everything was just on automatic and running—until the batteries would go out. Science can prove almost anything nowadays, so one can reasonably say that nature is an energy or system that was created and then set into motion. When bad things happened, I took it as proof of this. Bad things happen because the Creator created this world and then left. Sometimes, the world seems like a mess, doesn't it? Otherwise, how else would you explain evil people? The pain of good people? Babies born into bad situations? And the big one, of course: the Holocaust? How about COVID? I understood that evil is in the world because one has to choose good, but why did I have to suffer at the hands of other people's choices? Why did the Creator not protect me?

For a long time—looking back, it lasted for years—it was clear to me: the Creator must no longer be here, and that is why another human can hurt me, or my nation, or anyone.

I really struggled with this and felt a sense of abandonment: How dare You create us and then leave us to deal with the mess? Better not to have been created! Who needs this? I thought You wanted to give me good! I made the right choices, others didn't, yet I was receiving bad!

Then I had two (and later, more) personal revelations that changed my viewpoint. One was more impactful, but with time I realized just how pivotal the second one was for my life. I am sharing the first one, although very personal, because I truly believe it happened to me so that I can share the lesson I learned. I am sharing the second one to show you an example you can relate to—and then go on to discover one in your own life. The goal is for you to own your own story, not just read mine.

My first revelation was big. The following story is a raw depiction of a difficult time period in my life: a complicated birth, and my struggle with a pregnancy I was not prepared for. I realize this may be triggering—even upsetting—for some to read. I don't want to in any way diminish the pain of others who struggle to have children or who suffered from miscarriage.

This is my story, full of my experiences and realizations. I wanted to include this section because it was a critical point in my life that changed how I felt toward God.

When I was in labor with my second child, my son, I was in a difficult place. My family lived far away. The pregnancy was unexpected and came very soon after the birth of my first, a girl. Marriages have ups and downs, and I was struggling with a lot. At the time, my husband's grandmother was sick and there was a lot of stress in the family. He had just taken a job that took a lot of time away from us. In general, I was feeling overwhelmed. Sometimes, I just wanted to run away.

Then the labor started. After having an easy birth with my first, I walked in with no fear. That was a big mistake. From the very start, everything went wrong: he was three weeks early and upside down. They had to turn him (ouch) and then induce me (double ouch). They went to give me the epidural, put it in the wrong place, and I had a seizure (triple ouch). I was not allowed to eat or drink while in labor (which took thirty-six hours).

We finally got to the last part of labor...but I simply couldn't do it. I felt myself push too hard, I felt myself bleed, and I felt myself lose consciousness. I was hemorrhaging and they couldn't stop it. I was, literally, dying. In fact, I did clinically die before they were able to stop the bleeding and bring me back.

People always ask what I saw during that time, and I am always happy to share because it opened a lot of doors for me. I felt like I was falling, free-falling into a deep dark pit. But it wasn't scary. It wasn't a hole.

Indeed, it was warm, cozy, and safe. Most of all, at the bottom, it seemed there was a thin black blanket, and if I could only fall through it, waiting for me on the other side was something incredible. I felt a special light radiating from there, complete and unconditional love, safety and acceptance. To put it simply, I felt like I was falling into the biggest, safest, warmest hug in the universe. I wanted to get there.

I knew I was dying, and I was okay with it. I had been struggling so much in life that I was in a really bad place; I honestly (though foolishly) thought that my husband and kids would be better off without me. But then I heard my husband asking me to please come back. Drawing strength from the acceptance below me, I forced myself back (I actually remember telling myself that I'll die later, when he is not around).

I gave birth to a (relatively) healthy baby, but my struggles weren't over, and it took a while for the pieces to "come together." After my son was born, I went through a very difficult time period. I was emotionally and physically traumatized from his complicated birth, and I was diagnosed with severe postpartum depression. In addition, at the time, my daughter was only nineteen months old, and caring for my two babies was way more than I could handle. My parents lived thousands of miles away. I was plagued by migraine headaches, consumed by negative thoughts, couldn't get as far as the bathroom on my own, and my husband was working three jobs at the time. My marriage was falling apart;

my life was a mess. And in addition to my misery, questions about life and God and purpose tormented my thoughts.

Gratefully, through all this distress, I maintained an awareness that all was not completely lost; those moments of security I had found during the birth had stayed with me. When my day would spiral out of control, the memory of my birth-near-death experience would come to me. When both kids were crying and I was too weak to get out of bed, I remembered it. I remembered it and somewhere deep inside, I knew that there is a God. And that even after everything I was going through, I could trust Him. I knew I could trust Him because He had been there to "catch me" with complete acceptance when I was at my absolute low-est—when I had basically lost the will to live.

When my son was eight months old, I was two months into therapy, three months into this book journey, and finally starting to feel like myself again. I even had a clean house!

But then I found out I was pregnant.

For most people, this is happy news. At that time in my life, for me, it wasn't.

Everything just crashed down. I couldn't breathe. The trauma was still fresh. I absolutely adored (and still do!) my son and my daughter. I wanted to be the best mother for them possible. I felt that having another baby would take me away from them. Even more, the doctors were clear: There was a risk that I may not survive the birth, and they strongly recommended that we consider abortion. This was way too much for me. An abortion? How could I? But what if something terrible happened again? What if went through with the birth, and then I had PPD again? How could we possibly deal with another pregnancy and birth? Physically? Emotionally? My husband and I were at a complete and total loss. I didn't know what to do. I felt I had nowhere to turn. I felt desperate and trapped.

Then it hit me: God put the baby there. Someone said it to me in passing, "This must be good since God did it." I had quite the opposite reaction. The person who said it was trying to help. Instead, I got mad: "I never asked for this! I didn't ask for the overwhelm, the health issues, the third pregnancy. This was all the Creator's fault! I have so little family here, my husband is never around, PPD was awful, I almost died last time, and I can't handle this!"

As angry as I was at Him until now, this pregnancy felt like a betrayal. I literally started screaming. I had not prayed in years. I had not talked to Him in years. Yet here I was—in my room, literally, out loud, crying to God. I sobbed and cried and ranted and raved. Bawling and shouting about how unfair He was. How He had put me through the traumatizing birth, through the horrible past six months, and here He was with another blow. It was too much.

I cried and yelled until I tired myself out. I looked up at my bedroom ceiling in complete resignation and said to God, "You know what? I can't handle this, I'm giving it to You, You deal with it." And I went to sleep.

I woke up to a miscarriage.

Something shifted inside of me that day. I realized that the Creator is present and active in my life. We can never understand His ways. Sometimes what seems good is...not...and what seems bad is...not. Our human understanding is so limited. I don't know why I got pregnant and I don't know why the baby didn't survive. But I do know that God was and is active in my life—and in all of our lives.

Why did I need to go through all this? Only He knows. Perhaps, without being placed in that difficult position, I would not have prayed and had the powerful and impactful realization that the Creator is always present. I needed to know that and to experience it firsthand.

Also, perhaps the lesson was that pain is not always intrinsically bad. I am an interior designer, and one of the first lessons we learned in lighting class was that a room without contrast will appear bland no matter what: *The shadows are what showcase the brightness.* Without shadow, we cannot see the bright or appreciate it. Yes, hard things happen in life, but they help us see the good and appreciate it when we have it.

We can ignore Him for years and then have a tantrum. We can pray three prayers daily, or just connect from time to time. No matter what, He is around, watching and helping. Waiting.

Though terrible and difficult, in a sense I was lucky to have had that experience: I got to see firsthand, with unquestionable clarity, that the

Creator is still around and involved. And because I did, I want to share that clarity with those who have not seen or felt it. It is for that reason that I am sharing this very personal and intense story. I want you to know that you too can experience the Creator's involvement in your life; you need to open your eyes and hearts to see it.

The second story I want to share with you is not clear-cut at all, and that's why I think it's important—to show how possible it is to see the Creator, if you only look.

As I mentioned, I grew up in very religious schools. I was treated quite unfairly in my schools. I had gone through a lot in my personal life, and the school system did nothing to support me through it. On the contrary, when I asked what were—looking back—honest, legitimate, and fair questions, I was thrown out. I spent a lot of years being angry, feeling like it was unfair that I had to go through what I went through. It felt like hardships were coming at me from every angle: home, school, social life, and I could not understand why the Creator had given me this life.

Ask me today how I feel.

I *love* where I am and where I am going. I even appreciate where I came from. I love what I have become from the struggles I have gone through. I can even pat myself on the back: I am an amazing mother and a good person. I gained all the skills I now possess through experiencing what I did. It could not have happened any other way! If I had not gone through all of my childhood, I would not be writing this book, and I would not be helping others! (Hopefully.)

I *had* to go through it, all of it, every single piece, in order to become the person I am.

A lot of people will say that the Creator did not have to make it that way. He could have made it less painful. Did I need to go through so many horrible nights of crying?

I've thought about this a lot. Honestly, I do not agree. If I would not have felt that anger or pain—all of it—I would not have asked questions. I would not have been passionate enough to be really open to the answers and to share my findings. And the only way to feel, to actually feel, is by going through it.

Our relationship with God is like the relationship of children with their parents. A child does not understand why a parent does what they do. My kids get mad at me sometimes, like if I need to change their diaper when they have a rash; it hurts them, but if I don't do it, it will hurt them more.

When going through experiences in our lives, we do not see the whole picture. Although it took years, I finally did see the picture of my childhood, and I now understand why it had to be exactly that way. If I would not have been lit on fire, I would not have any fire for the passion of this book and more. I am now grateful for my experiences, negative and positive, because they shaped me and helped me create the change I hope to make.

Furthermore, I was never abandoned by the Creator at any point, even though I often thought I was. When I look back, I see that there was always somebody who I was able to turn to. I was never completely alone; the Creator made sure of that.

My father is a prime example.

My father, Rabbi Yaacov Haber, is fond of saying, "Twenty years tells the story." In other words, we do not know everything, but the Creator does. If we trust that, we will eventually see—twenty years later, five minutes later, or after we pass on to the next world—exactly why it all had to happen. But even more so, we will realize that the Creator is involved in our day-to-day lives. There is no way that all the little intricacies that made me who I am just happened by coincidence. One bit harder and I would not have made it, one bit easier and I would not have cared. It was too perfect to have been coincidental.

There was no abandonment; that whole storyline is wrong. The Creator watches me—and you—every day, and He is here, involved, every second. And I am sure if you look back at *your* life, you can point to a few moments or instances where it was clear there was something or someone taking care of you from behind the scenes.

But what if you do not see that? What if you really feel like the Creator is not involved in your personal life?

So now that I established for myself that the Creator did not create us and leave us alone, I needed something concrete to solidify that feeling inside of me. This is a personal journey, but I wanted to make it apply to everyone, and feelings don't necessarily prove anything. I started doing research. Let me share with you some of my conclusions.

CHAPTER 2

# THE WORLD

s I researched further, I learned a fantastic idea.

How do we know that the Creator is involved in the nitty-gritty details, in the day to day? We learn it from the *Ramban*,[1] who teaches that if we look at the history of the Jewish People, we see a lot of miracles.[2] Some were big and obvious to most. However, if we open our eyes and hearts, we will see a myriad of small miracles that the Creator does for us every day. Like a baby's heart beating for the first time, and that same baby instinctively knowing how to nurse, like you swerving out of the way at the last second when a car runs a stop sign, and countless other examples large and small.

However, for the majority of us who find it hard to see the small miracles, the Creator performs a big miracle every once in a while—as a kindness to those of us who need the extra nudge. For example, the State of Israel has survived against all odds, including the miracle of the Six Day War, when Israel was greatly outnumbered and still won. While the IDF is very effective, do you really think it is "natural" that a few million Jews can survive against hundreds of millions of enemies? In addition, the fact that the Holocaust didn't annihilate the Jews is miraculous! (Though why it happened is a valid question.) Huge nations have done everything in their power to end our existence, but Jews are still here. Greeks, Babylonians, Egyptians, the Final Solution. There is only one explanation: the Creator must still be involved on some level.

---

1   Rabbi Moshe Ben Nachman, commonly known as the *Ramban*, was a Spanish Talmudist who lived from 1194–1270. He was a leading Kabbalist (learned in the secrets of the Torah) as well as a philosopher and physician.

2   For further proof, the book *Crash Course in Jewish History* by Ken Spiro is an excellent resource.

My question then became technical. If the Creator is infinite and not bound by the constraints of this world, how is it possible for Him to be involved in this world? How can something infinite interact with something finite? Even with the *Sefiros*, how does that bridge actually work?

Before we can answer that question, we need to take a minute to understand the concept of "mystical Judaism," or Kabbalah. According to Yerachmiel Tilles:

> *Kabbalah is the ancient Jewish mystical tradition which teaches the deepest insights into the essence of God, His interaction with the world, and the purpose of Creation. The Kabbalah and its teachings, no less than the Law, are an integral part of the Torah. They are traced back to the revelation to Moses at Sinai, and some of them were revealed even before.*[3]

Rabbi Aryeh Kaplan explains further. The word Kabbalah means to "receive," implying that it is transmitted from person to person. This was indeed the case for a long time, until Roman persecution got so bad it was almost lost, and a select few *tzaddikim* wrote it down in "code" to save it. (By writing it in code, it would still have to be taught person to person and would not become widely misused.) The Torah has many levels. Some are more revealed, while some are deeper and more secretive. We need Kabbalah to understand every nuanced level in the Torah. Without it, we can understand a lot—but not everything. With it, we can understand everything that the human mind can possibly understand. While this is still limited, it helps us understand and connect to the Creator and the ultimate goal of life.

There are three aspects to Kabbalah:

- The theoretical, which is a description of the spiritual realm and worlds. This is the aspect of Kabbalah most commonly taught and learned.

---

3   Chabad.org.

- The meditative, which tells you how to actually get into that spiritual space and navigate it, something only a select few are able to do.
- The practical or "magical" Kabbalah, of which our knowledge is limited; no one today practices it.

Now that we understand what Kabbalah is on a very basic level, we can use some of the simpler teachings to help answer some of our questions. We can now explain how the infinite interacts with the finite through the Kabbalistic concept of *tzimtzum*. But first, let's take a minute to discuss the idea of a projector, which will give us a frame of reference for understanding it.

When a person wants to take a small image and display it in large, they place a slide containing the image onto a projector. The projector then takes the image and, by shining a light through a small lens, projects the image onto the wall across from it on a much larger scale. We end up with a large image on the wall that is condensed into a small version of it on the projector slide. This image on the wall is created by light, which—depending on the size of the wall and its distance from the projector—can appear as large as we like. In a sense, it is kind of infinite.

Now, imagine, on a greater scale, that the Creator is the light and the world we live in is the small image. The Creator squeezes the infinity of the light into the finite slide on the projector. We live in this world, which is a "limited version" of God's light, and therefore He is intrinsically involved in every tiny little detail. It is as if He *is* the world. The actual light going from the wall into the slide is the essence of the image—this is *tzimtzum*. In our analogy, the image is our world.

Therefore, it is almost as if the world is a contraction of the Creator's infinity. This is a mind-boggling thought that no one can completely comprehend. However, what we *can* understand is that the Creator is intrinsic to the existence of the world every second.

In the example above of the projector, let us think about the "controller," the one who places the slides on the projector. If this person were to make a tiny dot on the small slide, it would create a huge dark space on the wall. In the same vein, if they were to color in a blank part of the slide, they would create a huge piece of art and beautify the image.

So, who is this person making the marks that are impacting the light displayed on the wall in a big way?

It is me and you! It is each and every one of us. Our impact is that great! We are able to create amazing changes in the world based on our actions. We were given the power to co-create with God in that way, and that is one of the reasons we have free will—so we can be creative.

We learn in Kabbalah about the messengers, or angels, who bring the Creator's blessings into this world, and our actions and prayers up to the worlds above, closer to God. What we send up directly impacts what is sent down. So, if we color something beautiful on that small image, it is sent to the large image on the wall and directly impacts the light being constrained into the projector.

The Creator created the world, but we have the option to do with it as we please. To an extent, of course, we are placing the slides on the screens. We can even take it a step further and say that through our actions and prayers, we are writing on the slide and it reflects on the wall—literally changing Creation. How amazing is that?

This helps us understand the power of creation and prayer being given to humans. We have the power to change things in Creation. We see this in action when Avraham was given the power to bless in *Parashas Lech Lecha*.[4] *Rashi* explains that up until then, only God was able to bless humans and possessions, but now this ability was given to Avraham—and to humanity as well. This is merely an example of how some of the power of creation was given to humans.

Blessing is a form of creation; it is making something bigger, or more plentiful. This in itself is proof that the Creator has given a partial power of creation to humans. Some have more of this creative power (Avraham), some less (me)—but we all have it.

So yes, the Creator is involved in every minute detail. We can see it in our day-to-day lives if we open our hearts and eyes to see the miracles. We can see it in our generational miracles that He performs for our benefit. We can see it simply in the fact that we are still here, after every

---

4    12:2.

kind of persecution, with no logical explanation. We are, after all, the most exiled, persecuted, and detested nation in world history. Yet we are the oldest. How did we survive, when thousands of other nations didn't? It is not natural. It is supernatural.

If we need more concrete evidence, we can understand it through *tzimtzum*, which explains how the whole world is an extension of God. He is intrinsically part of every inch of the world. He is the light the world is created from and is therefore inherently involved in every detail. We can also appreciate that within that, He has created the ability for us to co-create or change His creation. Within that, He made space for us.

Once I understood this well, my next question followed: We can co-create and change creation, to an extent, but what exactly is that extent?

Rabbi Aryeh Kaplan explains in *Inner Space* (a fascinating book you really should read):

> *An interesting way to think about this is a computer system that changes the traffic lights from red to yellow to green. The computer has a system that sends signals to the lights to change when they should change. However, there are also sensors on the lights sending signals to the system if traffic is backed up. The system will respond in kind, keeping a light green for longer by the backed-up road.*
>
> *Same in our world. The Creator has an ultimate goal for the world and will send down what is needed with the angels for us to achieve that goal. However, when those same angels go back up to the spiritual worlds, they bring with them our actions and prayers, and those actions and prayers affect what is sent back down. We can affect our own destiny and fate. The Creator allows us that power of creation.*

It is important to note one thing: All the systems and signals do not affect the man sitting at the computer screen. And, if he wishes, he can override the system and do what he pleases. The Creator has the power to override what we are sending up and what the natural order of things will be. He doesn't usually do so, because that would take away our free will—but He can. We saw this in Egypt when the Creator hardened

Pharaoh's heart. Yes, usually we have free will, but in the case of this wicked ruler, nature needed to be manipulated in order for the Jews to leave and experience that as a people. When there is something much bigger at play, God takes the reins directly and makes sure it happens. However, 99.9 percent of the time, He leaves it up to us, so to speak.

Now, with that in mind, if you try to kill someone whom God doesn't want killed, He won't let it happen, because this would affect His ultimate plan. You might act, and even see the consequences of your actions, but if that person was not meant to die, they will not die.

So, while we have the power to create our own destiny, we also have the comfort of knowing that the Creator would not let anything happen to us that was not supposed to happen.

But then I got scared, which led me to another question.

The world is constantly being created, constantly being beamed into our projector, right? We know that the Creator is constantly there, facilitating the sunrise, making the earth spin, nudging our hearts to beat. This means that technically, the entire universe is in the Creator's hands and if He so wanted, we could be thrown or crushed or completely destroyed. We could be shut off. As we have seen, the coronavirus was a micro proof of this. Terrifying!

Until you realize that we are not crushed. The Creator keeps on sustaining us and has kept us functioning for thousands and thousands of years. We are here because of that! The biggest proof is that our heart keeps beating. There is nothing in our bodies making our hearts beat. The Cleveland Clinic explains that the oxygen-filled blood comes into the heart and the "bad" blood leaves the heart—but what is keeping the heart opening and closing its doors? The Clinic says an "electric impulse." And what generates the impulse? A spontaneous action by the pacemaker. Spontaneous or the Creator? Same thing to me.

There is no real reason the heart should keep squeezing, keep thumping, keep moving the blood, keep beating. Except for one reason: that the Creator is making it do so. That is my proof that the Creator is still involved, and not just involved but wants me alive and will keep me safe. Every morning that we wake up with a beating heart, we thank Him for it and express gratitude for his faith in us that he gave us another day on earth. Yes, He can technically shut the world off at will, but He hasn't and won't because it would stop Him from being the Ultimate Giver. It would defeat the purpose of creating the world.

So, the Creator did not create the world and then leave it all up to nature. He is here every day and every second.

Look around in your life, you will find times when this becomes obvious.

When my husband's grandmother was told she had one month to live and lived for another twenty years, we understood. When my friend was told she would never have children and became pregnant naturally when she was forty-two, we understood.

There is an incredible story about the Baal Shem Tov who was walking under a tree and saw a leaf fall. He turned around and explained to his students how this shows our Creator's love for all his creatures. Seeing their confusion, he picked up the leaf to reveal a caterpillar underneath. He explained how for one little caterpillar the Creator commanded the angels to command the wind to make the leaf fall to protect the caterpillar from the sun.

In all these instances and so many more, we can feel that the Creator loves his creations and is still here.

Interestingly, we can even see the continued involvement of the Creator in the exact theory many try to use to prove that He doesn't exist: evolution.

The Darwinian theory of evolution ("natural selection") does not negate the idea that a Creator was the first cause for the world. It doesn't even claim to explain how something came from nothing. Rather, the theory claims that cells slowly evolved into more and more advanced creatures, based on what they needed to survive.

A well-known evolutionary example is the finch on the Galapagos Islands. There was a time of serious drought, and the finches were in serious danger of starving. Over a number of generations, the beaks on the finches slowly got longer and narrower, enabling the finches to dig deeper in the crevices of the rocks and find food. Some claim that the biological changes that occurred were proof that the ability for adaptational change is hardwired into creatures, suggesting that all creatures could have developed by themselves, without a Creator. However, it is just as plausible—if not more so—to interpret it the other way! This is proof that there is a Creator and He is so involved that when he saw a small group of birds on a faraway island, He enabled their DNA to know how to change their beaks to slowly elongate instead of letting them all die out!

The cycles and rules of nature are sometimes seen as proof that the Creator is not actively running the world. However, let's think a little deeper. Think of nature as a type of kindness. Imagine if we did not have nature. We would never know who would wake up in the morning, where food would come from, or if we are currently safe in the place we are standing. Nature tells us what to expect instead of constantly living in the fear of the unknown. That is the Creator's kindness. Of course, this does not mean that "unnatural" things do not happen, or that we can know exactly what to expect for the rest of our lives, but it gives us a security that would be hard to live without. The Creator shows Himself through nature—its dependence, its wonders, and its beauty.

It does not mean we always *feel* His presence. Sometimes we feel abandoned, sometimes we feel tortured; we are tested in our faith. However, if we know and remember deep down that we are loved and cared for, we will know that what is happening is for our best.

Of course, this is easier said than done. I know.

And it naturally leads to the question of whether the Creator knows *me*. Even if He exists, and even if He sustains the world every day, does He care about me specifically?

We say in our daily prayers, *"Ha'mechadesh b'chol yom tamid maaseh bereishis*—He Who recreates every day the workings of creation." We learn from this that God creates the world anew every morning. As we established above, He did not simply create and leave; He recreates every morning and is committed to this world and to us. Rabbi Raphael Aron, in his book *Spirituality and Intimacy*, compares this to a marriage. He explains how just like God "wakes up" every morning committed anew to creating the world, so too, a couple should wake up every morning committed to their relationship. The system of nature and time is one of love.

I want to take this a step further. This couple wakes up every morning committed to the relationship, so long as there is faith in the relationship. Much the same as the faith God has in humanity, a husband and wife must have faith in each other. As soon as there is no longer faith and love, the couple wakes up uninterested and uncaring. They do not recreate their marriage. They go their separate ways on their separate days—until eventually they separate for good. Only the couple with continued faith and love wakes up committed to the relationship.

The same goes for our Creator. The mere fact that He recreates the world every morning is a demonstration of His love and faith for us. The fact that He recreates your personal world and is committed to it not falling down around you—that is an expression of His love.

Yet, there are times when we go through our personal form of pain and crisis. We feel like the Creator has not shown "commitment" in keeping the world stable and firm for us and that He has allowed our world to crumble around us. This is a valid feeling, which many can relate to—myself included. Sometimes it really does feel as if we have been abandoned. One thing that helped me overcome these feelings was to work on creating a foundation during the stronger times, when I felt myself in a safe and happy place. When everything is going well, we can forget to work on our faith and recognizing the source of our blessings because faith seems easy then. It is in precisely those times that we need to create the strong foundation we will be able to lean on when things feel unstable. Later, when the dark times have passed, we often find ourselves able to see how the Creator was there all along, even if not immediately. Either way, if we build a foundation in which we fully believe that what happens is for our best—that the Creator really and truly wants to give good to us and that we do not always understand what is good and what is not—we will know it so deep in our bones that we will be able to access it even when the world seems to be crumbling around us.

It is important to note that most people do not have unshakable faith; it is a level that is incredibly hard to reach. However, if we surround ourselves with people who have strong faith, they will help us—and together we can have unshakable faith. I am fortunate to have my husband, who has reminded me over and over again that at the end of the day, the Creator is wiser than me, knows more than me, and that I should and could trust Him.

Find yourself someone who can hold you up when you are having a hard time believing that the Creator is good, and that He loves us. It is not just love, though; more than that, He believes in us.

Think about it. Imagine you were the owner of a start-up company. Starting a company takes hours and years of hard work, sleepless nights, mistakes, tears, failures, and occasionally, wins. But many, many people are willing to do all this, and more. Why? Because they believe in their business, and that it will all be worth it in the end.

The Creator does the same thing. He forgives our mistakes, keeps us going, gives us everything we need and more, because He believes that our contribution to the world has tremendous value. How does God have so much patience for us? He believes that the end result will be worth it all.

If that is not a reason to wake up in the morning, what is? This is why we say every morning, "*Rabbah emunasecha*—Great is Your belief." Rebbe Nachman explains, great is His belief in us, that He woke us up to another day.

We can go further and ask: Why create us and love us?

Kabbalistic works teach us that originally, the world consisted only of the spiritual World to Come, and in it was the treasury of souls. The spiritual world is composed of levels. Some of the souls are damaged or blemished due to reasons we are not privy to (whether from past lives or perhaps even before the physical world was created). The Creator wanted to give the souls an opportunity to repair themselves, to enable themselves to rise to higher levels in the spiritual worlds. He therefore created a world of "doing"—a world in which we can actually change ourselves for the better. That is this world.

When we want our child to receive an education or learn a profession, we send him to school; similarly, the world we live in is a "university" for our soul. Our hope is that by the end of our lifetime we will be able to fix and uplift whatever needs fixing and fully enjoy the World to Come.

Now, when a parent sends their child to school, they don't send them alone or stop loving them. They send lunch, little notes, and are always there to advocate for them and make the experience as positive as possible. The same goes for us. When the Creator placed our souls in this world, He did not stop loving us. On the contrary, He loves us more than we can imagine—and worries and watches to see if there is any way in which He can help.

Imagine a little boy running in the playground and being too wild. He falls and scrapes his knee. What happened here? We might say he was being "punished" for being wild. Or we might say this was a natural consequence. But whichever way we look at it, the fact is that from this experience he learns that being wild can result in injury.

Everything can be a lesson if we let it be. The more we let lessons teach us, the more we fix ourselves so that we can truly enjoy the World to Come, and even our time in this world. We need to remember that the Creator is loving and caring, and not looking to hurt us—nothing that happens to us is really a punishment per se.

We can change the word "trauma" to "lesson." It makes you see everything in a different way. In other words, whatever happened did not happen *to* you, it happened *for* you, to teach you something. This is not necessarily a religious idea, and it is a fundamental mindset shift that has helped me get over numerous things in my life.

So why are we here? Mainly, to refine a piece of our soul that needs to be completed. When someone needs to refine a part of themselves, they go to university. They identify their strengths, the areas of knowledge through which they can channel the passion and potential they were born with, and become a professional in that area. Some like to say this world is like a jail, but jails rarely *help* the prisoners. Jail is where we put someone dangerous so as to keep others safe—its purpose is not to refine the person. This world is not a jail; it is a university where we all can grow. As it says in *Pirkei Avos*, this world is just a hallway to the next; we are merely preparing ourselves.[5]

God created us and the world, and He placed us here for the sole purpose of elevating our souls, of making ourselves better so we can better

---

5   4:21.

enjoy the World to Come, the ultimate world of receiving. By working for it, it becomes part of us, and we "enjoy" it more both in this world and in the next.

But how do we know how to refine ourselves? We are not directly told what to fix, and we cannot usually understand all these little lessons and messages.

How do we know if we are walking in the right direction?

What if we've gone to university but are in the wrong classroom?

Well, for that we have the Torah.

CHAPTER 3

# THE TORAH

At first glance it can seem like the Torah is a bunch of stories with some rules thrown in or learned from hints.

In reality, it is much more. The Torah is a guiding light for the humans on earth. An instruction manual, if you will. We believe that God created the world and He created us in it. He then told us all the secrets to achieving our potential in a book called the Torah, and he gifted that book to the Jews.

Speaking personally, if I am going to take on a tremendous number of rules and laws (613 to be exact)—and some of them are not easy!—I would want to know that this book is the actual word of my Creator. I want to know that this is what I need to do to achieve my perfection.

So how do we know the Torah is directly from the Creator?

There are many fascinating and powerful explanations. One way to know this for certain is that He revealed Himself to six hundred thousand men (almost three million people in total) and these people passed the experience on to their children, who passed it to their children until today. There is no way a lie of that proportion could have survived even one generation. Someone, somewhere (or more likely, lots of people) would have gotten up and said, "This is all some big lie! Why are you telling your children this? How dare you tell *our* children that God spoke to us when we all know He didn't." In other words, we know it is true because an entire nation witnessed the revelation and passed it on for generations.

No one is asking us to believe that one man had a revelation, and then the group of believers grew. No one is asking us to believe a group of five people who claim they themselves saw miracles and proof. Nope.

Other religions make these claims, and it is no wonder they aren't so convincing. In our case, the entire nation was privy to this special event because it was for the entire nation.

The nation did not believe—they knew. And they passed that knowledge and memory on to their kids, who told it to their kids, and so on and so forth. It is important to know that Judaism is the *only* religion in world history to claim national revelation. Every other religion claims one person who had a revelation, and a few people who believed him. Their group of followers ultimately grew until it developed into a religion. Judaism is the only religion whose entire nation witnessed the revelation and told their children about it. Why didn't others make such a claim, seeing how powerful it is? Because it is impossible to lie about it. We're the only people to claim it since we are the only people it happened to!

We have established there is a Creator. We have established that this Creator is all-knowing and intelligent. According to what three million people saw, this Creator chose Moshe to come up on the mountain and bring down the *Luchos* (tablets). He then told him to write the Torah and commanded the Jewish People to keep that Torah. Do we really think that this amazing all-knowing Creator would have made a mistake? Would He have let Moshe change his words? Or even just make a mistake? No way. If Moshe had written the Torah himself and pretended the Creator wrote it, the Creator would have gotten rid of it! Moshe had to have written the actual word of the Creator because the Creator would never have allowed him to spread a man-made Torah out to the Jews in His Name.

There is another proof that the Torah had to have been written by the Creator of the universe and no one else. Rabbi Dovid Sapirman discusses this in his book, *Emunah: A Refresher Course.*

Numerous times in the Torah, facts are cited that were not yet known to mankind at the time. For example, the Torah writes that we can eat any animal that chews its cud and has split hooves. It then goes on to detail exactly which animals in the world—four, to be precise—we should be aware of since they only have one of these signs, not both. At the time the Torah was written, not all the continents had been discovered yet, and there were still many species of animals that were not known. Yet, in all the centuries since the Torah was given, no animal other than those four has ever been discovered to have one sign and not the other. How could any human have predicted that? Only the Creator of the world could possibly have known that!

That is just one example, but there are many more that bring similar proofs. This helps us believe that the Torah was a gift from the Creator and was not man-made. But how do we know the Torah is a guiding light by which we should live our lives?

Well, since we know the Torah to be true, we can look inside.

When we read the rebuke in *Parashas Bechukosai* and *Ki Savo*, we see that the Creator brokered a kind of "deal" with his creations, specifically, the Jews. He says:

> If you follow My laws and faithfully observe My command-
> ments, I will grant your rains in their season, so that the
> earth shall yield its produce...and the trees of the field their
> fruit...if you reject My laws and spurn My rules, so that you
> do not observe all My commandments and you break My cov-
> enant, I in turn will do this to you: I will wreak misery upon
> you—consumption and fever, which cause the eyes to pine and
> the body to languish; you shall sow your seed to no purpose, for
> your enemies shall eat it.[1]

In other words, God promised the Jews that if they keep the Torah and follow its guidance, He will raise them up to the top of the world. They will be a nation of nobles and a holy people. From this we learn that following the Torah has positive results.

But what if I don't care about being the best nation in the world, and I just want to live my life? Believe me, this thought has crossed my mind more than once.

The *Sefer Hachinuch* explains that the only reason we have been given the Torah is so that we may do good.[2] For once a human does good, he

---

1    *Vayikra* 26:3–16.
2    16:2.

opens the path for good things to be sent to him. As we learned above, by choosing good, we resemble the Creator and can receive the ultimate good and everything in between. We also know that what we send up impacts what is sent down. By choosing to do good, we will receive good.

All God wants is to be able to send good things to people. This is why He created the world. But how can we choose good if we do not know what is good? For example, if someone asked us which is better, chocolate or broccoli, and we did not have the knowledge that broccoli is healthier, we would likely choose chocolate. The Creator realized that we needed guidance to know what is good and what is not. Therefore, He wrote a book, telling us the secret of how to live in a "good" way and this way, and we can make the choice to do so. This allows Him to send us all the good in the world. It is a symbol of His love for us and His desire to only do us good.

We do not have to keep the Torah, but it is a privilege, and it's the smart thing to do. In other words, keeping the Torah is not simply something I "have to do"—the more I understand, the more I *want to* keep it because it enables me to live the best version of my life and reach my purpose.

But why so many details? It seems almost trivial to have to pay attention to so many small details. Sometimes it can even deter you, especially if you are already a spiritual being and feel connected to God without them.

Rabbi Adin Steinsaltz explains that rather than thinking of Torah laws as tiny unimportant details, think of them as an orchestra. In an orchestra, every single instrument does something different and is equally important. Yet, if you were to take one of these instruments and play its part alone, you would get bored pretty quickly. If you look at the orchestra as a whole, you can see the beauty of each individual instrument.

It is the same with the Torah. Each mitzvah in the Torah fulfills a special job in how it refines us and makes us better people, closer to God and to goodness. When taken out of context, the details may seem repetitive and boring, but you have to look at all 613 mitzvos at once in order to see the beauty of the individual.

We can apply this to the Jewish nation as well. If you ever feel insignificant, the Torah tells us just the opposite is true. Every soul in the Jewish nation is assigned a letter of the Torah. Just like every single letter is needed and there are no extras, every single Jew is needed and there are no unneeded Jews. In addition, every Jew corresponds to a letter of the Torah, proving that the Torah belongs to every single Jew. It is ours, a gift to cherish as if we were standing at Har Sinai ourselves. (Incidentally, many say that all Jewish souls were there, so in a sense, we were.)

Let's look at the mitzvah of mezuzah for example. It is a mitzvah to place a mezuzah on the post of every doorway in your home.[3] Many even have a tradition to kiss the mezuzah whenever they pass through a doorway. This may seem trivial and repetitive. Why not just kiss the mezuzah only when we walk in and out of the house? Why not just once a day? But *every single time* we walk through a doorway?!

While it does seem repetitive, and people can do it without thinking (we're just humans, after all!), the point is to subtly but regularly remind us that God is in every single room and that He is with us and protecting us. Reminding ourselves of that in a small way puts us in the right frame of mind so that whichever room we are in, we know: He is there, so act accordingly. In the bigger picture, it makes a huge difference.

When we add all this up, it begins to make sense. I remember thinking, the whole thing is indeed logical. However, I remember feeling…despair. How am I supposed to feel enlightened and special with so many restrictions?

Many people have a problem with the Torah. They say the Torah is supposed to be a source of enlightenment and freedom and positive light—but how is that possible when there are so many restrictions, and it can feel like the laws are consuming us?

We can see this clearly with one mitzvah in particular: Shabbos. This is supposed to be a day of rest and relaxation, but instead we are faced with

---

3   With the exception of bathrooms, etc.

thirty-nine things we must not do. Each of those items are subdivided into lists of even more things we cannot do. Then we have all the things we have to do, like eat and pray, and so on. From the outside, it seems so restrictive! Yet, if you ask anyone who keeps Shabbos they will tell you that it's the most relaxing day. Why? Because through the restrictions comes a freedom we would otherwise never have. Once you start compromising, you see a drastic difference in the relaxation and freedom of the day. This is because the restrictions actually protect freedom.[4]

I began to consider how the "restrictions" of the Torah are not necessarily restrictions at all. That's not their point. And kept correctly, it's not even their effect. They are boundaries that allow us to reach our full potential without getting lost on the way.

We have established that the Torah was written down by Moshe and is the word of the Creator. We have established that the Torah will help us reach our ultimate level of good and teach us what good is. And we have established that it was written with love and with eternal messages.

If the Torah is so great, why did God not give it to the whole world? Why only the Jews?

Well, originally God's intent was to give the Torah to mankind. The world was created for the human, not the Jew. As we learned above, God wanted to create humans, and He created the world for humans to be able to live in, and the Torah for humans to be able to make good decisions. Nowhere does it say that this purpose was only for the Jews. On the contrary, in *Parashas Bereishis* it says the world was created for the sole purpose of the Torah being given and its laws being kept.[5] However, when it came time for mankind to accept the Torah, only the Jews accepted it, and therefore, only the Jews have it. Considering how amazing it is, why would anyone reject it?

Probably the same reason you, me, and many others have been or are hesitant about keeping the Torah: it is not a passive book. You can't just have it to look at when you feel like it and throw it away or ignore it when you don't feel like it. You need to accept it in its entirety to enjoy

---

4    We will go deeper into this in chapter 8, "Shabbos."
5    1:1.

it correctly. This is why the Jews, who were the only ones to accept it completely, were the only ones who received it. That being said, the gates are not closed. If someone wants to be part of the Jewish nation and is found to be absolutely sincere, they have the option of converting to Judaism and receiving the Torah as well.

Let's recap what we've established until now:

- The Creator is good, and He created us to give to us.
- In order to allow us to be the ultimate receiver, we have to have free will and the ability to choose good.
- Once we choose good, we receive good. How do we know what "good" is? We look in the Torah.

But let's say we look in the Torah and we do not understand what is written. Either it is vague, seemingly impossible, or illogical, or sometimes even seems to contradict itself. How do we make sense out of the Torah when we do not understand it?

As holy as they are, words are...just words. They can be misunderstood. Just like we need to sit in a class to learn a textbook, we need explanations to truly understand the Torah. For this, God gave us the Oral Torah. When Moshe was up on that mountain getting the Ten Commandments and the Torah, he was also being taught the Oral Torah. The Creator took forty days to teach Moshe the explanations of the Torah, so he could guide the Jews to keep it in the correct way. When Moshe came down from Har Sinai, he wrote down the Torah thirteen times, gave one to each tribe, and put one in the *Mishkan*. Then he set up a Sanhedrin, a court of seventy wise men, and taught them the Oral Torah, the explanation. If a Jew had a question or was confused about something in the Torah, they would ask Moshe or one of the seventy wise men.

What do we do today? We read the books of Chazal, the rabbis from previous generations, and the rabbis we have today. Many, many books have been written with answers to almost any question you can think to ask on Torah, and some you did not even think of.

However, the question arises: Do the rabbis commenting on and explaining the Torah have the same power as the Torah itself? Do I need to follow what a rabbi says the same way I need to follow what the Torah says? It is hard to believe that mere humans, no matter how exalted and smart they may be, can make decisions and rulings that I have to listen to, with the same credibility as the words of the Creator Himself! This question bothered me for years.

I also had many questions around the vocabulary the rabbis use, which I found very confusing. Whenever we are talking about the practical application of the Torah in our lives, many different descriptions of commandments come up. We have terms like halachah, *minhag, das Yehudis,* and more. What do all of these terms mean?

So, while we understand that the Torah is true and valid, I wondered where we stand when it comes to the commentary and explanations. So many questions come up here:

- Who, and what do we believe?
- How can we trust any human being to explain God's Torah?
- How do we know whom to follow when two rabbis say different things?
- Are some rabbinic rulings more binding than others? Does it make a difference who said it?
- What happens if/when a rabbi says something I find completely ludicrous?
- Do I need to care about the explanations at all? What kind of implications do these scholarly understandings have on my life?
- Can I ignore the rabbis and follow only the Torah itself through my personal understanding?

Let's try to make sense of all this and answer these questions—and more.

CHAPTER 4

# THE RABBI

I t is important to take a moment here and talk about the halachic process and the traditional way of deciding what is and isn't allowed in our religion. As I was learning the above concepts, I started feeling that the Torah was very much something I believed in. Deep down, I knew a Creator had created this incredible world, and He wouldn't have just abandoned us without telling us how to live. Yet I felt less sure about the books written by rabbis, like the Gemara or the *Shulchan Aruch*. I felt that I did not necessarily agree with their conclusions and wondered, do I *have* to agree with them? More so, do I have to follow what seems to be merely their opinion?

To answer this, let's learn about how the Torah was given and what happened from then until now to bring us to where we are today. A bit of our history needs to be very clear. This is the base of our heritage I mentioned above in the introduction.

In his introduction to *Mishneh Torah (Sefer Mada)*, the *Rambam* explains the entire process from the time the Torah was given until his lifetime:

The Torah states the following three things God gave Moshe on Har Sinai:[1]

- *"Luchos ha'even"*—the Ten Commandments
- *"HaTorah"*—the written word
- *"Ha'mitzvah"*—the explanation of the Torah (Oral Torah)

Now you may ask, why does the Torah need an explanation? Why didn't God just write it in a way that would be easy for everyone to understand? Imagine you went to college for a class that you knew

---

1    *Shemos* 24:12.

absolutely nothing about, with no context or background information at all. If someone handed you a textbook and expected you to understand it all just from the textbook, you would have a very difficult time. The ideas and concepts would be completely foreign to you; you would need a professor to teach it to you. The Torah was a completely foreign concept to the Jews. Even the Avos (forefathers) didn't have it! Yes, they kept parts of it, but it had not yet been given to them in full (had they had the complete Torah, they would have known what would happen to them and thereby lost their free will).

From the moment the Jews became the chosen nation, they needed to understand what this completely new and foreign concept entailed. The Oral Torah (the explanation) was absolutely necessary, and still is to this day.

Let's be honest: Have you ever tried reading the Bible in English? These words are not in my vocabulary, and I am sure I am not alone. It is so hard to understand. It cannot be understood simply by reading it. Explanations are necessary. Therefore, the Creator gave us the textbook and explained it to Moshe verbally. When Moshe came down as the "professor," he was repeating verbatim what the Creator told him. That is the Oral Torah—the Creator's exact words to Moshe.

Moshe comes down from Har Sinai and writes the Written Torah down thirteen times. He gives one to each of the twelve tribes. He then places one in the *Mishkan* right next to the *Aron* that has the broken *Luchos* in it. Then he teaches the Oral Torah to Yehoshua and the seventy elders.

A few questions here.

Why did Moshe not write the Oral Torah as well? Why not put down the explanation exactly as God said it for eternity? This would have saved a lot of questions, confusion, and arguments. Second, who were these seventy people, and why did Moshe not teach the explanation to the whole Jewish nation?

The reason Moshe did not write the Oral Torah down is trifold:[2]

- First, we gain merits every time we study and try to figure out

---

2    Heard from Rabbi Yaacov Haber.

the Torah. Moshe did not want to take that opportunity away from us.

- Second, the Torah is not meant to be robotic. God gave it to us *"l'asoso*—to do it." It is not a passive book; it is a working book that we use and learn from every day. The Creator wanted our contributions and discussions. He wanted us to choose the Torah every day, not blindly follow its words like sheep. The Jews were expected to learn, understand, and come to their own conclusions, while keeping within the set of thirteen parameters (one of the lessons taught to Moshe).[3]

- Third, the Torah is eternal. However, the messages in the Torah need to be applied in their own way to each generation. If the explanations were written down and set in stone, there would be no room for the growth and evolvement as a nation that was needed to complete the ultimate goal of the world. Therefore, Moshe did not set it in stone. Instead, he taught it orally and explained the concepts so they could be refined and applied to each generation.

This helps us understand why Moshe did not write down the Oral Torah, but who were the seventy elders he taught it to? Why did he teach it to them and not the whole nation?

The Torah concepts Moshe was teaching his student Yehoshua were the exact words the Creator had told him. These words and explanations are called the *mesorah*, tradition. It was a sacred gift given to Yehoshua to pass to the next generation without changing a single thing. From this *mesorah* the Jews would know what to do, and if there ever was a question, they could ask Yehoshua to help them understand.

In order to keep the integrity of this gift that was given to one person at a time, a system had to be put in place. We had to make sure that not a word was changed. Therefore, Moshe gathered together the seventy wisest men of the nation and created a "committee." This committee (the Sanhedrin) would learn the Oral Torah as well, and they would be

---

3 These thirteen parameters were eventually written down by Rabbi Yishmael ben Elisha and added into the Gemara as a *beraisa*, as explained below.

responsible for ensuring that when Yehoshua eventually passed it on to Pinchas, not a word would be changed. Having a group of men who knew the original version would stop anyone from changing even a single word. The applications may change, the understandings may change, but the explanation God gave to Moshe will never change.

Once the Jews were living in Israel, Yehoshua led them with his knowledge of the Oral Torah while simultaneously teaching it to his student Pinchas, who took over after Yehoshua. Pinchas taught the Oral Torah to his student, Eli. This is the same Eli who, if you are familiar with the story, saw Chanah praying for a child and thought she was drunk. When Chanah explained herself, Eli blessed her with a son who would be great, and whom Eli himself would teach. This child grew up to be Shmuel HaNavi, one of the greatest prophets of our history, and he was the next holder of the *mesorah*. Shmuel passed the Oral Torah to King David, whom he enthroned, and David passed it to Achiyah HaShiloni.

Achiyah, incidentally, was alive during the time of Moshe but was still a baby. The *Rambam* points this out to show that each holder was not an entire generation, rather a short time period; the seventy elders would see many holders throughout their lifetimes, thus ensuring that it was the same *mesorah*. If one of them passed away, he was immediately replaced, creating an overlap through each link in the chain. This way they really did make sure nothing was changed from the original word of God.

After Achiyah came Eliyahu HaNavi, who passed it to Elisha, and so on, until they got to Yirmiyahu. He was the last prophet, and he witnessed the destruction of the First Temple. The Jews were sent into exile and dispersed among the Diaspora. However, the tradition still continued, and Yirmiyahu taught Baruch Ben Neriyah, who taught Ezra.

At this point, Ezra identified a problem. He realized that with the spread of the Jews all over the Diaspora, the seventy elders could no longer answer all the questions. Therefore, he expanded the "committee" to 120 elders and called them the *Anshei K'nesses Hagedolah*. These 120 men were sent to different capitals around the Diaspora to lead the different communities of Jews. Incidentally, one of them was Mordechai, and that is when the story of Purim happened.

The tradition continued until seventy years later, when everyone was able to come back to Israel and build the Second Temple. At this point, everyone from the *Anshei K'nesses Hagedolah* had passed away, besides for Shimon HaTzaddik, who became the only holder of the Oral Torah.

Take a deep breath. That was a lot of history at once. So far, we have seen the Creator give Moshe the Oral Tradition, and Moshe passed it to his student. It passed from student to student, along with the committee, until the rebuilding of the Beis Hamikdash, where we have one remaining committee member, Shimon HaTzaddik.

Shimon HaTzaddik led the Jewish nation as they rebuilt Jerusalem and he became the Kohen Gadol (high priest). As the nation settled back into routine, he wanted to continue the tradition of passing down the *mesorah* as it had been told to Moshe. However, there were a few problems.

For one, many people came back from exile with different variations of the Oral Torah, as each rabbi understood, taught, and applied it in slightly different ways. Each community had applied the teachings differently and many were confused. In addition, there was now the added problem of not having the Sanhedrin or the *Anshei K'nesses Hagedolah* to ensure nothing changed.

So, Shimon HaTzaddik set up a new committee of seventy wise men and taught all of them the *mesorah*. Then, instead of teaching one student at a time, the explanation would now be passed down in duos, so that each one could keep the other one in check, further ensuring the integrity of the Oral Tradition. They also wrote down *Pirkei Avos*, which included basic guidelines of how one should behave. They now had a guide of the basics of a Jew's behavior.

The last thing they did was apply the thirteen principles of passing a law, which had been taught to Moshe. They passed a law that anyone who retained a custom from exile would have to validate it in the following three ways:

- They must be able to trace their understanding of the tradition back to Moshe, meaning it was taught to them by a rabbi who was part of the chain.

- The tradition must follow all thirteen rules and fit the parameters that were handed down from Moshe.
- The tradition cannot contradict the Torah. All of these conflicting applications are merely understandings of the original explanation given by God. If it directly contradicts the Written Torah, it is false.

It was during this period that multiple groups of Jews were formed, all of them with authentic traditions. So long as their tradition fit the three parameters set down by Shimon HaTzaddik, it was considered a true Jewish custom. There isn't just one way to be a Torah Jew.

We can understand this concept by talking in modern-day terms. When a person grows up in a certain community and finds that their soul does not connect to that particular *mesorah*, they might "stray." After searching, they might find that a different community, equally accepted in Judaism, is more meaningful to them and enables them to connect to their Creator more deeply. Many fine Jews have done this. Litvaks have responded to their souls and become Chassidic, Chassidim have "found a new rebbe," and so on. This must be done with tact and understanding—but if a person feels unfulfilled, it is the correct thing to do. That person has searched for and found their soul's path!

Sometimes, family members don't view it this way, and see such a change as an abandonment of tradition. However, the tradition that one must hold dear is the tradition that was given to Moshe on Har Sinai and passed down. How each community applies it, understands it, and adds to it is up to them. If my goal is to connect to Torah and mitzvos, and I am not thriving in my current community, there is nothing wrong with "finding my own path."[4]

In this way, original tradition was passed down, pair to pair, with the seventy wise men. This went on until the time of Rabbi Yochanan ben Zakkai and his counterpart, Rabbi Shimon ben Hillel. In this period, the Jews were under constant oppression in Jerusalem, so the learning centers were moved to Yavneh, where the Sages continued to study.

---

4   We will discuss what this means in relation to halachic matters that include *das Yehudis* in chapter 6, "Modesty."

However, it became difficult to keep the Oral Torah intact. There were wars and plagues and confusion. During this time period, all of Rabbi Akiva's students died, and multiple claims on variations on the tradition became rampant. It was getting very difficult to keep the straight line of tradition.

Along came Yehudah HaNasi. He was a direct descendant of Hillel, counting seven generations between them, father to son. What is amazing and important to know about this family is that they were all holders of the tradition. Hillel lived before the time of great confusion and had a clear understanding of the *mesorah*. He taught it to his son, who taught it to his son, and so on. This created an unbroken chain of teaching, so that the surrounding confusion did not affect them. Yehudah HaNasi learned the exact same explanation that was taught to Hillel, which was the same one since Moshe.

However, Yehudah HaNasi realized that passing on the tradition orally had become unsustainable. Worried about the quality and clarity of the Oral Tradition for generations to come, he came up with a solution. He gathered the notes of every holder of the tradition from Yehoshua until himself, and compared them to what he knew from Hillel. He clarified each piece using the three rules we stated above and came out with the original, pure Oral Torah that was given to Moshe. He then wrote it down so it would not be lost. He called this book the Mishnah.

But how could he have written down the Oral Tradition if we learned earlier exactly why not to write it down? The answer is that the Torah was at risk of being lost, and Rabbi Yehudah HaNasi understood what needed to be done. Still, he didn't fully write it down—he kept the Mishnah cryptic. It is hard to understand, and it still needs to be studied, or else it will cause confusion. However, there is no longer an argument about what the Creator told Moshe. There are differences in how we understand it and how we apply it to our lives, but that is all; the basic Oral Torah is written down clearly in the Mishnah.

It should be noted that Yehudah HaNasi was not the first one to write down the orally transmitted tradition. Rabbi Shimon bar Yochai, in the time of Rabbi Akiva (second-century CE) took it upon himself to write down the mystical part of the Oral Torah while hiding in a cave from the Romans. The tradition that was transmitted from Moshe consisted of four levels. There was *p'shat*, meaning the simple explanation of the written word, and this is what Rabbi Yehudah wrote down as the Mishnah. However, there was also *remez*, *d'rash*, and *sod*. These are the more mystical parts of the Torah, the Kabbalah. This was written down in the *Zohar* by Rabbi Shimon bar Yochai earlier.

We see here that the Kabbalah was also passed down, however more secretly. Only a few individuals received it in each generation, and it was not explained to the masses so it should not be misused. Rabbi Shimon bar Yochai was concerned it would be lost and wrote it down cryptically. The *Zohar* is an incredibly difficult book to learn, and can only be learned with someone who has learned it through the chain. It still requires oral transmission, but there are cues to keep track of the material so it doesn't get lost—cryptic notes reminding the teacher of the lesson. Today it is possible to learn the *Zohar*, but most of us can only understand it on a very basic level.

Let's summarize. God gave Moshe the Written Torah and with it the Oral Torah, the explanation. It passed from Moshe, master to student, all the way until Shimon HaTzaddik, and then passed down in pairs until Rabbi Yehudah HaNasi. The Temple had been burned to the ground, the Jewish nation was weak and persecuted, and the tradition was at risk of being lost. Rabbi Yehudah took the notes of every student-turned-master in the chain, and put them all together in a book called the Mishnah. Rabbi Shimon took the secret parts and wrote the *Zohar*.

Rabbi Yehudah HaNasi had eleven students who helped him put together the Mishnah. After it was completed and was being learned at large by the Jewish nation, these students became the teachers who taught the Mishnah to the students in yeshiva. They were called the Amora'im. Besides explaining the teachings in classes, they wrote down books with the explanations.

In order to make sure the Mishnah was understood and remembered properly, the rabbis set up a rigorous system to make sure only the truth was passed on. Any opinion needs to include proof that a teacher said it, and it needs to date back to Rabbi Yehudah, or further back if possible. An opinion also needed to be logical and come from a reputable person.

Nothing could contradict a Mishnah, and all had to fit into the thirteen parameters referred to above. These are just a few of the processes they put each idea through.

However, three hundred years later, it was getting hard to keep track. Rabbi Yochanan, one of the leaders of the time, took it upon himself to gather all the books and notes written to explain the Mishnah, and he wrote down the *Talmud Yerushalmi*. This included just the summaries and final decisions of the rabbis, not necessarily all the arguments. The arguments were still well known orally and were talked about, so he did not see a need to write them all down.

At this point there were places of learning all over the Diaspora. Students were studying the Written Torah, the Mishnah, and the *Talmud Yerushalmi*. Torah was spread all over the world and many great *roshei yeshiva* lived during this time period. Any notes that surfaced during their time period from previous holders of the Oral Tradition had to be proven through all the conditions stated above.

The last of the leaders of this time period were Rav Ashi and Ravina. They were two of the greatest scholars of that time. Toward the end of this era, they felt the confusion and dispersion rising again. In order to preserve the Oral Tradition, they took the Mishnah, teachings from the *Talmud Yerushalmi*, all the arguments of the leaders of the generations, the *Beraisas* (notes and parchments found during this time from previous generations), and the books that were written on various topics, and they put together the *Talmud Bavli*. This is what we call the Gemara.

An interesting point to note here is how vital the dispersion was to our evolution. Because we were repeatedly separated and persecuted, we were constantly checking, evaluating, and perfecting the transmission process. If not for all the confusion, which ultimately led to all the solutions, we would not have evolved as a nation; we would have stayed in the same place spiritually and developmentally as we were then—an infant stage. We needed all this to evolve and become the nation that eventually will greet Mashiach. The dispersion and persecution, in effect, spread Torah all over the world and forced us to constantly reevaluate. It was terribly difficult, of course, but the silver lining was that it forced us to be extra careful. A kind of clarifying perspective, in my opinion.

Eventually, the Jewish world split into two major parts, Ashkenazic and Sephardic. Each one was subdivided into small communities all over. There was no unifying mass media then, and they were physically distant from each other. The leaders of different communities understood the arguments in the Gemara differently, and since there was no Sanhedrin, there was no one to decide who was right. In other words, each community developed their own set of customs, many overlapping, all correct, but each set only binding to its own community.

After the split a new rabbi came along called the *Rambam*. The *Rambam* was one of the greatest sages in Jewish history. He felt the need for clarity. He decided to write down the outcomes of the Gemara, excluding all the discussions before and after. He called this book the *Mishneh Torah*, and he dedicated its use to those who needed to know the practical halachah (the conclusion of what is permitted and prohibited according to the Torah). This book was created for those who needed to know the final halachah, but did not have time to read and understand all the arguments before the conclusion. While this helped many people, some rabbis were troubled by his innovation. They pointed out, accurately, that the Torah was meant to be worked with, not dictated, and its practice dynamic, not robotic. However, there was a need for a simplified version, and the *Mishneh Torah* eventually became widely accepted across the entire Jewish nation. It is important to note that while we take it as a valid point of transmission and summary, it is not totally binding for Ashkenazic Jews.

This process of refocusing conversations into a simple version happened several times. After the *Mishneh Torah* was expanded on and many books were written, Rav Yosef Karo wrote the *Shulchan Aruch* summarizing all those comments and writing out the bottom-line halachah we hold by. Years later, the Chafetz Chaim summarized and elucidated, compiling the *Mishnah Berurah*. This was really the last commentary whose rulings were accepted universally. From there, rabbis from different communities summarized what has been taught since.

While not binding for all Jews in all communities in the same way that the *Talmud Bavli* is, the *Mishneh Torah* and other summaries are used in the process of determining halachah today and are widely accepted.[5]

So, now that we know what the *mesorah* is and the different pieces of the puzzle, when we want to know the halachah, how do we find it?

The first step is to find the source in the Torah—the actual *pasuk* it is derived from. Then we look and see what the Mishnah says to explain it. We now have the absolute basics of what we should do. We then check and see if the rabbis in the Gemara explained it further. We are not done though; we keep looking to see if the subject evolved further. We check to see if the *Rambam* or *Shulchan Aruch* talk about the topic and what they say. Do they expand on it?

Once we have all that clear, we can check what our specific community does. Personally, the rabbi I follow, Rabbi Moshe Weinberger, recommends that each person should do an internal check to see what they feel is the correct thing to do after learning all those steps. The idea is to try not to be robotic, and rather use our intuition. This is one of the main reasons we chose him as our rabbi. But that is my community, and while intuition is very important, so is what our community does; let me explain.

This is where *das Yehudis* comes in. This concept refers to societal norms. It is the code of conduct for a Jew and differs depending on when and where one lives. Exactly what one is and is not allowed to do regarding *das Yehudis* was never written down because it inherently changes. It is simply what is considered appropriate in the community in which you live.[6]

Now that we know what our tradition and heritage is, and that we come from an incredible unbroken chain, we can delve into understanding its nuances.

After much research and thought, I was comfortable with the system in theory and the history that has kept our tradition solid. Yet, I wondered:

---

5    I cannot go into full detail as this is not a history book, but I highly recommend Ken Spiro's book *Crash Course in Jewish History*.

6    We will discuss this further in chapter 6, "Modesty."

What makes a rabbi today authorized to discuss and transmit these ideas? Now that I had increased my understanding, I questioned, what makes someone a leader today?

If we no longer have the master-to-student relationship like we did with Moshe and Yehoshua, what makes someone able to dictate halachah or discuss their understandings of the Gemara?

In other words, what really makes one a rabbi?

It seems to me that rabbis can be divided into two groups: those who lead and mentor, and those who make halachic decisions. These two roles overlap, but they involve two separate responsibilities.

Let's look at a rabbi who makes halachic decisions. This must be an extremely learned person. Their job is to know all the practical halachos. However, more than that, their job is to understand the nuances, and the basis for decisions, so that they can accurately decide the law for each specific situation. They must understand the deeper message and how it has evolved, and apply it to their generation, as we learned above. This kind of rabbi does not need to know only the final word, but the whole train that led to there, so they can make a learned, educated ruling that will not hurt the person they are trying to help.

This is a lofty goal. Rabbis like this study for many, many years before receiving certification (*semichah*). They must be learned in all aspects so they do not err in their decisions. Because of this, many rabbis will choose a niche and focus on that or learn one area at a time. For example, the laws of Shabbos, then the laws of kashrus, then the laws of *niddah*.

While technically speaking, to become a "rabbi" one needs ordination, there are always going to be individuals who did not receive official ordination but are widely known as knowledgeable and wise, and so they take on leadership positions. On the other hand, there will also be those who, while they did receive official certification, are not knowledgeable enough to be entrusted with the safeguarding of the tradition. It is our job to make sure we are asking someone we trust, who knows the *mesorah*, the tradition we spoke about above.

Regarding the rabbi who operates as a spiritual guide, what makes this kind of person trustworthy? What is his actual job?

It's hard to describe. It is like explaining what a *tzaddik* does. This is someone who leads with love, who is there for his followers when they need him. An extremely righteous and Torah-knowledgeable individual who can lead the community with wisdom and heart. Someone like the Lubavitcher Rebbe, Rabbi Avraham Yitzchak Kook, or Rabbi Ovadia Yosef. Such righteous souls are lofty and close to the Creator, and they help with their wisdom and experience. This is a tall order. Who and how is one worthy of such a title?

The answer will be different for everyone, as such a person has to be someone you can relate to, whom you can easily and comfortably talk to. Additionally, included in what God told Moshe on Har Sinai was that the rabbi must be accepted by the community. In today's terms, according to Rabbi Moshe Feinstein in *Igros Moshe*, the "community" would mean a large group. Alternatively, he must be endorsed by a recognized rabbi or organization. It is important to get references and make sure the person you are speaking to is a good person and a worthy mentor. Beyond that, it is up to you and your gut, or better yet—your soul.

If we choose to, when we have a question in life, we can ask our spiritual mentor for guidance. (Ladies, please note: this spiritual mentor does not have to be a man. If a woman is wise, and learned in the tradition, she can advise you just as well.) But I still wondered, when we have a question in halachah, are we obligated to ask a rabbi?

In our discussion of the Oral Torah, we saw how Moshe wanted the Jews to be actively involved—Judaism was never meant to be mindless. We are commanded to choose it every day with every action. If we mindlessly follow someone else's thought process, we are not choosing anything; we are brainwashed. We must always think for ourselves.

However, the fact is that we do not know all the answers. Sometimes, we simply don't know what to do in a given situation, or we may have a difference of opinion with our spouse, for example. When this happens, we can call the rabbi (whether the mentor or the *posek*, or perhaps the same person for both). We then ask them for their opinion based on their extensive knowledge of Talmudic history and halachic law.

Sometimes, you might want to ask for sage advice, but not necessarily a halachic ruling. Is there such a thing as asking a halachic question in a way that does not require you to follow the answer? Many people do this, others wonder if this is permissible, and many refrain from doing so altogether. What is the right way?

I think there is a deeper question here.

Ideally, when you ask a rabbi a question, it should be *after* you have done the mind work. You've thought the issue through, but simply cannot figure out the right thing to do, as established above. Essentially you are saying, "I want to do the right thing, but what is the right thing?" And what happens if you don't "like" the answer?

Here is where it gets into an even deeper conversation. Making sure your rabbi is the right one for you. This relates to both the spiritual mentor and the halachic rabbi.

Many times, a woman will ask her questions to her husband's rabbi, or the rabbi from her childhood. Sometimes a couple will use the closest rabbi in their neighborhood. But these choices might not necessarily be reflective of their soul.

Every Jew has a unique soul with a unique purpose. We were brought to this world to accomplish a certain goal, and that goal needs different tools than another person's goal. Add to the variations of souls and goals the fact that there are so many different ways to interpret the Torah. Each soul resonates with a different path. We have many sources for this, for example: "*Chanoch la'naar al pi darko*—Raise a child on his own path,"[7] which insinuates that there are multiple paths. Above, when we spoke about the variations in law and custom that arose when the Jews returned from exile after the First Beis Hamikdash was destroyed, we noted the same. We learned that anyone who can trace back their tradition to Moshe, and it is consistent with the thirteen parameters, his tradition is valid. This created multiple groups within Judaism, and we need to discover which explanation, which process of understanding, is most true to our soul. What do we innately feel is the truth—our truth? This is not to be confused with choosing whatever we want to do and

---

7   *Mishlei* 22:6.

going with that. It takes immense honesty to be able to say what we feel is true—not what we think is easy.

This raises another question: Can a person just jump from group to group?

The answer is, of course not. Finding one's place in Torah is not a casual decision to be made or unmade on the spur of the moment, and there are guidelines. Traditions are valid as long as they go back to Moshe Rabbeinu and fit into the thirteen principles of the Torah. Many people find themselves connecting to a tradition that differs to that of their father—perhaps connecting with how a different rabbi understands the Torah, or with a different Torah approach that speaks to their soul. Once they do the inner work—and make sure to choose a legitimate community and follow its customs in all areas—they can belong to any accepted community that speaks to their soul.

We see many children who grow up in Modern Orthodox homes and become Chassidic, because their soul needs some more fire. We also see many children who grow up Chassidic yet ultimately find their place within the Litvish community. The main thing is that any change must come from an authentic, sincere place.

Since we have each come to this world for different reasons and goals, each person's soul will be pulled in a different direction. Some souls will be pulled toward a more structured practice of Judaism, where everything is well-defined, with a focus on halachah and clear parameters, as this gives a sense of order. Some people will be pulled toward God-centeredness and spirituality, with little interest in the material world. Others will be pulled toward the loving and forgiving version so they can help those at the bottom of the spiritual ladder. When we understand this, we can then discover to which direction our soul is leaning. Once we know that, we can find the group of Jews (and it should be a group that is substantial and accepted by Torah Judaism at large) that most fits our soul—and commit to living by its philosophy, principles, and also the halachic conclusions of its leaders. By virtue of our chosen commitment to the path that is true to our soul, we can live fulfilled lives, following the halachic rulings and customs of our community, even if that sometimes means stretching a little beyond our comfort zone.

When we do find our place, it is *our* place, and others may choose differently. This is important to point out, as we do not judge our fellow Jews for the path they chose. We are all doing what is correct for our souls, and we need to respect each other. Whether we agree or not with the way someone else is practicing Judaism is not our problem. Remember, it is between them and God, and our job is to respect and love our fellow Jew.[8]

This is a big undertaking, and it does not take a day to figure out. It requires work, but it is worth it. As an example, my husband grew up in a more mainstream home. When he went to yeshiva, some of the rabbis taught Chassidic teachings, and he felt drawn to these. He looked further into this direction, and eventually discovered Rabbi Moshe Weinberger. He felt that when the *rav* spoke, he spoke to his soul. The *rav's* words simply resonated with him. He found his community and that is where he stayed. He calls Rabbi Weinberger whenever he finds himself in a dilemma and is not sure of the correct thing to do. My husband now lives a life different from the one he grew up with and has found his own soul's path. He loves the teachings of Rebbe Nachman and the Baal Shem Tov. Yes, his *rebbi* is Rabbi Moshe Weinberger, but he draws inspiration and learns from many other rabbis, and from those who have passed on as well. He found (or created) his place in Judaism.

If you are happy and connected where you are in Torah, that's great. Don't change a thing. However, if you feel stuck, uninspired, or lost, perhaps you can try to do what my husband did—expose yourself to different Torah teachers and see what works on a "soul level" for you. Once you have found your community, you won't feel such a need to ask questions in the way we mentioned earlier—without intending to follow the answer—because the answer will feel right to you every time.

I heard a good suggestion for finding your place from one of my mentors. She suggested formulating a question about an area of your life and asking respected spiritual mentors about it. Find them online, in

---

8    *Vayikra* 19:18.

videos, or ask friends. When you speak to someone who truly makes you feel like this is the right answer—someone who speaks to your soul and who you can relate to—you know you've struck gold. If you feel like they are approachable and they get you, stick with them. Remember, you are not looking for someone who is necessarily charismatic or famous; you are looking for someone you can feel comfortable talking to, who understands you on a deep level, and whose answers make sense to you in your soul. Someone who you can connect to.

Now, this is going to be difficult because finding the community truest to you can be a journey—and it requires a lot of honesty to not just choose the easiest version. Harder still is if the community you connect with ends up being different to that of your parents or friends, who might not be as accepting as you would like. But when you know you are living your truth and doing the right thing, you can hold your head high until the whole world catches on. It does not make it easy, especially if the community you come from is not accepting—even alienating—of those who leave.

If you can stay in your community and find meaning, connection, and inspiration, by all means do so. If you can't, and you need to go elsewhere in order to connect to Torah and mitzvos, do it. It is a journey everyone has to go through on their own. Open conversation and mutual respect are a must on this road, and finding people to support you is important as well. Staying in the community you are in is always an option as well—I know some incredible people who, though it wasn't always easy, chose to stay in the community they were raised in. Having weighed the pros and cons of leaving versus staying, they are happy with their decision and are able to live their truest selves within the parameters of their community.

This is not an easy journey, and I wish everyone the ultimate clarity and strength in finding themselves. As I was going through my own journey, my husband agreed to write about the process from his point of view. I think this account could be meaningful for couples who are going through a similar situation and help them understand one another. Two people won't always be on the same page, and I loved the way my husband spoke about it:

Shmuel is a graduate of the *semichah* program at Yeshiva University, which means that after many years of learning, and being a dorm counselor and role model for yeshiva boys, he became an official rabbi. For several years we lived in Brooklyn, where he did an amazing job as the rabbi of a shul. Afterward, we moved to Pomona, where he continues to study, teach, and advise many young men. This is Shmuel's take:

> *When navigating a marriage with hashkafic and religious differences it can feel like one was cheated. Yes, in many ways it's a lot simpler when you are in similar places with similar goals. However, this is not a prerequisite for a healthy relationship. Healthy relationships are built on mutual respect, trust, and support. Practically, this means a lot of compromise. It means talking about what is really important to each person, and then finding middle ground to work with. Speaking to each other, and communicating clearly and as things develop, is crucial. If one half of the couple wants to change something about their appearance, or in how they do something, it should be talked about. Think about why it's important, and convey that, find a way to do it in a way that works for both of you. Another crucial part to making this work is respect. Initially, when Kayla was going through this process, I had thought it juvenile. I was under the impression that everyone goes through this as a teenager. However, I quickly realized this was not the case and started to enjoy and respect the process. While initially I was nervous that Kayla would decide to be not religious long term, I soon realized that was my insecurity and should not matter. After that, it was an inspiring journey to watch. Yes, inspiring. Watching someone be so passionate about something you have taken for granted is an amazing sight to see. The care and the passion and devotion to research was incredible, and showed me that she cared more than anyone doing it all passively. In addition, it did not once make me feel like being less religious, or pull me down. We do not have to feel secure in our religiosity by making sure everyone around us is the same.*

*If we do, perhaps we should be going through this journey as well; another person should not be a factor in our relationship with God.*

*Another note I would like to make is that of divorce. Many have asked if we considered divorce during that time, and I absolutely did not. I feel that when divorce is a backup plan, it is always there in the back of your mind. Leaving just simply was not an option for me, and so considering it or thinking about it was not either. In addition, being embarrassed of the journey was not an issue as well. What someone else decides to do is not a reflection on me and vice versa. I truly felt that the people who actually cared about us in life would look past it, and those who did not, good riddance. Now, this can impact things like children's schools and living in a neighborhood, and those should be taken into account, but whatever she chose to do was her decision.*

Back to Kayla: I'd like to share something personal now. It isn't comfortable to talk about personal "things" in public like this, but it is important. During this time, I felt very alienated from my husband, but not because he alienated me—rather, because I alienated him. Every marriage has its challenges and they are much more difficult when one partner is struggling, as I was. I think that if one can learn to respect the other person (frankly, the way my husband respected my journey) then it can work, as long as you don't cross each other's red lines, and respect that there are two people on two paths. Done this way, I think it really can work.

This does not mean it's easy. There will be challenging moments—like when your husband wears a *bekeshe* you hate instead of a suit you love, or vice versa! But if you focus on the relationship and not the religion aspect of it, the important things make themselves known. Little else matters.

If you do decide to "switch" communities, it doesn't mean you need to cut yourself off from your family and friends. I have maintained (almost) all of my relationships even as I've changed countries and communities. My best friend is still the same best friend I've had since fourth grade. My parents had an adjustment period but are so proud of my growth. My siblings for the most part have accepted me, and I think that's because they realized I'm not going to try and change them or their kids—I'm just on my own spiritual path.

Can you please everyone all the time? No, but it all comes down to respect. If you respect them and they respect you, there is no reason you should not be able to maintain the relationship. There are many ways to connect to our Creator and His Torah. Don't judge others, and they won't judge you.

While switching rabbis and/or communities may be appropriate in some cases, it is not to be done lightly. And it is important to know the difference between shopping and switching. Where is the line between looking for an answer we want, and looking for the truth?

Honestly, this is something we each have to check for ourselves:

- Are you asking around until you get the answer that's easiest to implement?
- Are you switching rabbis every six months?

Make sure you are being true to your soul. And remember that it is not only the rabbi you choose, it's also your spiritual mentors and your social circle. It is important to have a social circle or group of friends that will build you up and bring you closer to the Creator. When we change communities, it usually means adjusting our social circles as well.

It is important to note here that the switch does not have to be black and white, or sudden. You can slowly and gradually find yourself; in fact, that is the healthy way to do it. Generally speaking, when someone finds their place in Judaism through a sincere search to connect to God, in a slow and healthy fashion, the outcome is normally more stable and long-lasting, and their loved ones are often more accepting.

Unfortunately, it is important to mention the sad—though, thankfully, rare—phenomenon of rabbis who have acted dishonestly or inappropriately. While the vast majority of rabbis are really trying to help, and do give so much, there are cases of rabbis who have done serious damage.

Don't let this sad reality affect your relationship to Torah.

Every "industry" has people who use it negatively. People are good, bad, and complex. There are doctors who corrupt the system, but that does not make all doctors evil. There are bankers who end up as major thieves, but that does not mean all banks will steal your money. Much the same way, there are indeed rabbis who abuse their power. However, they do not speak for the majority, and we cannot throw out the baby with the bathwater.

We must be diligent and make sure that the person we are turning to as our spiritual mentor is a very good person, and be careful who we allow into our lives. As with everything, we do our best in choosing who to connect to and that is all we can do. The rest is up to our Creator.

Now, the question all the female readers are waiting for, or at least I was: Why are all rabbis men? Is that cultural, halachic, or just plain wrong?

This brings us to our discussion of women in the Torah, female empowerment, and how we can understand Judaism in a non-sexist way.

Let's do this.

CHAPTER 5

# WOMEN

I n general, I believe that each person has their own unique set of talents and abilities, and regardless of whether they are a man or a woman, we should respect that. So, if she hates cooking and he happens to be good at it, who cares about preconceived women's roles? If she wants to be a stay-at-home mom and doing so makes her feel whole, she should. If he can't use a tool to save his life, and she loves building, is that a problem?

While working on this book, I received many questions and concerns from women about women's roles, *tz'niyus*, and other pressing topics that typically make them feel misunderstood, marginalized, and mistrustful of the Torah understanding of women. I wanted to address them directly from the sources and from my perspective, as a woman who relates to their struggles and feels the same way. It isn't always easy for women to get clear answers on challenging topics. The language of our sources can be complicated and sometimes seems harsh. When we ask sincere questions, we're too quickly called feminists and told "that's why women shouldn't learn Torah." This can be devastating to a young woman finding her way on her spiritual path—and can induce a feeling of "This is not my Torah."

While not every woman experiences this, I have seen it enough to dedicate an entire chapter of this book to discussing the Torah perspective on women. We will go through this logically, with sources, to understand and make sense of common concerns and issues in this area.

So, what kind of issues are we referring to? Through studying and discussing the many issues pertaining to women in Judaism, I have broken down the problem into two separate questions that need resolving:

- What did the Creator intend when He created me as a woman? Did He intend to make me weak and reliant on men or did He intend for me to be strong and independent?
- What does the Torah say regarding how men should treat women and regarding how women should carry themselves? While we all have negative and positive urges and attributes, the Torah instructs us on the best way to act.

Let's address the first question. What was the intention of creating men and women so differently?

At first glance at the makeup of society and the world, it seems that stereotypically, women were created weaker and men stronger. Women tend to be physically weaker, and many men seem to have an inherent—some might say primitive—urge to dominate us. We seem doomed to be attacked.

There is, of course, the positive spin on this: women possess a certain quality that men innately want to protect, and that is beautiful in its own way. Which woman doesn't love the idea of her husband protecting her?

However, we are here to ask the hard questions:

- Why would God have set things up in a way that enables women to more easily be exploited?
- Why not give women the ability to protect themselves?

The above questions are coming from the assumption that women are inherently weak, and this allows them to be treated negatively or taken advantage of. However, I'd like to suggest that we reframe our perspective and consider this issue from a completely different angle: an understanding in which the woman is not weak at all—just a different kind of strong—and she can very well protect herself. Through this understanding, we will see how a man who hurts a woman hurts himself. We will see how women do have the ability to protect themselves, and they certainly should, but not in the way we might have thought.

In order to thrive in this world, we need two different kinds of strengths. We need the aggressive, go-getter kind of strength that propels us forward, and we need the calm, inner strength that keeps us tethered, coolheaded, and ensures we don't destroy everything around us in our quest.

We can think of these two kinds of strength as follows: the aggressive strength is like an arrow pushing in the direction it wants to go, moving forward, while the calm, inner strength is like a circle, ever cycling back to the source, whole, and calm.[1]

The point here is that both of these strengths are admirable and beneficial, but neither reach their full potential on their own. The arrow shoots off, forgetting its source, and with no clear path. The circle is whole and calm but going nowhere. However, what happens when we put them together? The circle, combined with the arrow, creates a spiral. If it is a positive union, it results in an upward spiral; if it is negative, it leads to a downward spiral.

These two strengths are often referred to in terms of masculine and feminine. The calm, grounding circle is the feminine force, while the more aggressive arrow is the masculine force.

We each possess both drives. In other words, this does not refer to male and female as we know it. Furthermore, it certainly doesn't mean that those who are not married will not reach their full potential. Rather, it is speaking of a more general union of the masculine and feminine energies which, while expressed in a marriage, is actually much more basic to creation.

The Torah tells us that every soul is created *"b'tzelem Elokim*—in the image of its Creator."[2] This means that the Sefiros, the traits of the Creator that we mentioned earlier, exist within us, and it is our job to refine them. [3] Our Creator is beyond physicality and is not defined as male or female per se; rather, He possesses attributes of both—and therefore, so do we. Every human has both male (arrow) and female (circle) tendencies.

A woman may have more of a tendency toward a circle, with less of the male aspects, and vice versa for the man. However, we all have—and

---

1   Adapted from Miriam Kosman's *Circle, Arrow, Spiral: Exploring Gender in Judaism.*
2   *Bereishis* 1:27.
3   See chapter 1, "The Creator."

need—both forces. It is important to find the balance between these two energies inside of ourselves, both as a couple and in how we relate to the world. This partnership shows up over and over again, such as between us and the Creator, between the different parts of nature, and between the Jewish nation and the rest of humanity.

Why is it so important to find a balance?

A circle with no arrow essentially stays still. A Jew isn't meant to stay still; we are always looking to grow and to reach our full potential. We are here to accomplish the goal for which we were put on this earth. At the same time, an arrow with no circle leaves one ungrounded and with no control over the direction of its trajectory. Without being grounded, one will not last long. When we are trying to get somewhere—whether spiritually or physically—if we do it recklessly with eyes only on the goal, we are bound to forget why we wanted to get there or cause destruction on the way. If we approach the situation calmly and logically, we will neither forget our goals nor destroy them.

The male arrow and the female circle work together to create a spiral upward to the ultimate goal of spiritual perfection. If the arrow shoots off, abandoning the circle, that arrow will not be able to achieve its greatness. The same goes for the circle that tries to stop the arrow and keep it in the ground. Both are equally necessary and important—they just have different roles.

Another analogy for the unique interdependence of the masculine and feminine is a tree, with strength in its roots and trunk, as well as in its branches and leaves. Roots have no purpose without the branches, and the branches cannot survive without the roots. Of course, neither one is better than the other; both are necessary and require mutual respect from each other in order to work together.

A beautiful example is raising children. The ultimate goal is to raise children who reach their full potential, accomplish the goals they were put on this earth for, and make the world a better place. If we want a positive result, we need both kinds of energy: the arrow and the circle. Imagine if a parent only focused on the day-to-day realities of life with a child, or only focused on their future. One without the other creates an imbalance. We need to stay in the present and stay whole, while working toward the ultimate goal. We must make sure we are using both of our strengths—encouraging the child to go forward while at the same time creating deep, healthy roots. Both strengths are equally important and necessary.

Sometimes the circle analogy is interpreted as a demand for women to stay home and stay quiet. This is a difficult message for a strong woman to accept and can cause her to feel resentment toward the Torah perspective on gender roles. She may feel she's being treated unfairly or as an inferior. This is because she is not recognizing her potential in the world. It's essential to remember that the feminine aspects of being a circle, with calm, inner strength, are about the *soul*—not the *home*. Staying home or being a public figure has nothing to do with the feminine energy. If you have a gift or talent, share it! We are in this world to make it and ourselves better; being quiet and hidden is not the end goal. You have a purpose to fill. Go do it, while keeping your superpower—the ability to stay calm and grounded.

We must also remember that a couple will have both energies, and each couple will have a different balance that works for them and their specific situation. No two people will have the same distribution of energies, and they need to be in tune in order to fully reach their potential.

Rabbi Menachem Schneerson, the Lubavitcher Rebbe, explains the difference between men and women in a beautiful way. He points out how in today's society, we seek to take away all the differences between man and woman in the quest for equality. However, equality does not, and should not, mean the same. He brings the example of the brain and the heart—each one is vastly different from the other yet both are of equal importance to the body. If one of these organs should stop functioning, the body would not be able to survive. So too with the man and woman. They are not the same nor were they ever meant to be the same. They each have a different job and need to do that job in order for the body—the world—to survive.[4]

---

4   Heard from my mentor, Manya Lazaroff.

This is all very nice in theory, but in practice, young children need their mothers. It bothered me. Why is the woman expected to have the children *and* take care of them? It doesn't seem fair.

Rabbi Schneerson explains: The truth is that any man who loves and respects his wife will not let her work too hard, and that is actually his commandment—to take care of, and love his wife. However, this answer is quite unsatisfactory, since the majority of women are pulling more than their fair share of responsibility in the home. Why? God created the woman with an extra dimension of *binah* (spiritual knowledge). Most women are naturally more intuitive and empathetic because of this, and it makes them particularly suited to caring for a child's spiritual well-being. Since this quality is so vital, but often underestimated, God made sure young children are in "good hands" by putting them in the care of a human who has been endowed with these special values. This is, of course, a generalization, as there are many women who don't feel this innately—and there are many men who do. The Creator made each of us unique. But as a general rule, this is usually the case.

Nowhere in the Torah does it say, "Thou shall let your wife slave for you." On the contrary, if you look at any of the Torah giants in our history, you will see that they all had responsibilities in the home. Similarly, if you visit the home of any learned and righteous man, you will see his concern that his wife should not work too hard out of love and respect for her because he views her as special and holy.

It is true that many women feel that the Torah creates a situation in which the women is overworked and underappreciated. What with men praying three times a day, making time for learning, and being the ones in the forefront of all our holidays and life milestones, it seems as if women get pushed to the side, stuck with the mundane day to day responsibilities. In practice though, life is a partnership, and a husband and wife are meant to work together. In an ideal world, men would protect, respect, love, and cherish their wives. They would do everything they could to make sure they are not overworked, that they are appreciated, and that they are happy and fulfilled. Any man who does not support his wife emotionally, whether or not he uses the Torah as an excuse, is just wrong. The husband is there as her partner, to help her and support her. That is his role.

This leads us to the problem of how certain Torah sources speak about women. For example, when a man takes a woman from the enemy during a war, instead of being told that it is forbidden to do so, he is told to make her ugly. That sounds quite one-sided. I know this problem held me back, until I found an explanation that resonated with me; I want to make sure it does not hold you back as well.

There is an idea the Gemara mentions over two hundred times: *"Dibber ha'kasuv b'hoveh*—The Torah speaks in the present." What does this mean?

When the Torah was given to the Jewish nation, it was written to that generation, and they were the ones who had the hardest time accepting it. In a world where moral code was not popular, and the laws in this book were not easy to keep, Judaism was a completely foreign concept. The possibility for overwhelm was huge and the nation's ability to accept the Torah would have been compromised. Therefore, the Creator gave them the Written Torah on the level that they could accept it, but the internal messages are eternal. We understand the message from the Torah, not necessarily the literal words.

In other words, we must put things in context, and not try to superimpose our current morals and culture on a world that existed thousands, or even hundreds of years ago.

The Torah was given to one generation, which had to make the decision to accept it. This first generation blindly accepted a completely new and foreign concept, and took on ideas and practices that were far removed from what they and the rest of the world knew. The subsequent generations, having been raised in the ways of the Torah, were able to see its eternal value.

For that reason, the Creator uses language in the Torah that would not shock the generation that received it. This means, their culture and what they were used to was taken into account, so that it was something accessible to them. For example, if murders and killings were happening left and right for the most minor offenses, the idea of not killing anyone ever again would be too hard to accept. Therefore, the

Torah instead outlines situations when murder is and is not appropriate, and what to do if someone killed a member of your family. Then slowly, as we evolved, we understood what the eternal message was—to have humanity.

As another example, it says in the Torah that you must give your wife shelter. Why did it need to say this? Because at the time the Torah was given, this was not always the case at all. If the Torah would have explicitly said at its most basic literal level to treat your wife with complete respect, and love and honor her because she is your fully equal partner, it would have been beyond the grasp of many of the men at that time. That may be upsetting to hear, but it is a different issue for a different time. For now, we have to understand the existing circumstances of the time. Therefore, the Torah made use of its multidimensional meanings and layers. Some levels apply to some generations more than others. In this example, always be one step above the rest of the world. The rest of the world may well—and did!—use and abuse women, and then abandon them on the side of the road. The Torah says: Don't do that; marry her, give her a home, and feed her. In other words, be better. The righteous men of the time, and over time, more and more people in general, would understand the deeper levels of Torah pushing us toward even better behavior.

Now, once we have that mindset, we can go ahead and question what seems unfair in the Torah. Now, we can genuinely learn the reasoning behind it and not just accuse the Torah of being misogynistic.

Some mentions of women in the Torah can indeed appear negative. Common grievances include women not being able to give a *get*, not being counted in a minyan, and the halachos of *niddah*, among others. Let's focus on one example from the Torah.

The Torah tells us that if a man sees a woman in a field, and he attacks her and lies with her, then he must marry her or pay her father a sum.[5] As a woman reading this, I wonder, what about her wishes? What about his punishment?

---

5    *Devarim*, chap. 22.

However, the context is crucial. In the ancient world, once a woman had been attacked in this way, she would be abandoned, and no one would want to marry her. The Torah therefore includes this law in order to protect a woman. The Torah requires this man to take care of her—or provide the funds so that her father will be able to. If we learn this issue at a deeper level, we will see even deeper mystical and inspirational insights, but at its most basic level, we need to know that this was a *good* law for women.

When the Creator wrote the Torah to give to His chosen people, He wanted them to accept it. The whole point of existence is written in the Torah, and He knew that the Jews would need it as their guide. However, if the Creator would have explicitly written about the ideal situation—men and women as fully equal in their homes, with the women being treated as humans and not property—it would have seemed too out of reach for many men of that time period and would not have been accepted.

Therefore, the message was written in many layers. At its most basic level, the goal was that the Jewish nation should treat their women at least one level higher than the rest of the world. At a time when women were viewed as if they were on the same level as cattle and often treated as such, the Torah commands that you give her food and drink, etc. Nowadays, when women are treated as humans with their own emotions, feelings, and independence, the Torah demands to treat her with the utmost dignity and respect, and to cherish her. The deeper and more inspirational attitudes to equality came to light with the historic development of the world,.

This comes into play in other areas as well. When it comes to keeping kosher, the Torah tells us not to cook a goat in its mother's milk. However, we took that message and do not mix any kind of animal milk with any kind of animal meat. We even have separate dishes. The same goes for laws of Shabbos and laws of modesty. While the source is always in the Torah, the practical applications come from the halachic evolution that was mentioned above.

Let's take a moment to fully understand what that means. Can I take whatever message I want from the Torah and apply it to my life?

As we learned previously, before an idea is taken from the Torah and applied to our life, it must be within certain parameters. The practical application of halachah has to be within the general guidelines of Torah thought and practice, accepted by the majority of the Jewish nation, and the teachings must be based on a traditional link in the chain, with sources and logic.

Once we understand this, we can understand what the Torah was saying. The message was: To begin with, treat your women better than the rest of the world. The rest of the world "marries" women and abandons them. But you shall put a roof over her head, give her a *kesubah* that you must fulfill, and if you decide to leave, give her a *get* to make her eligible for other men.

During ancient times, if a man thought that his wife might have cheated on him, he burned her alive on the spot. No questions asked, no courtroom—he just burned her alive. In fact, he was often (unofficially) required to do so to maintain his family's honor. To change this, the Torah requires a man to prove that his wife acted wrongly and have a court decide if and what should be done about it. Today, of course, one cannot kill a woman for any of these types of transgressions, or any reason at all. We get divorced or go to therapy! We took the message and evolved.

We see in this example how throughout the generations, each concept was developed to be appropriate for the time. The ultimate goal is to eventually get to a place of perfection. Within the confines of Torah thought and practice, we progress in each generation until we reach the state of Mashiach and a perfect world. It is very important to remember two things:

- We cannot impose our standards on a culture that existed thousands of years ago.
- We are not at the finish line, and not everything is going to be perfect today; we are still evolving. We must keep this in mind when we learn any segment of the Torah and our heritage.

So where are we holding now? We understand what the Creator intended when creating two different strengths, and we see how the

Torah instructs the Jewish men to treat women better than the rest of the world does.

But do we see anywhere that the Torah specifically tells men to respect women? Why was the world treating their women so badly to begin with? And has this generation missed the message?

Women are still feeling the repercussions. It seems like every time anything goes wrong in the world, women are told to dress more modestly! Young girls are taught to completely cover up in order to protect men's thoughts (as if it weren't the responsibility of the men). Even the marriage roles in some communities are strict, and the wife must be submissive.

Once again, let's answer the first question first.

Through the story of Avraham and Sarah, we can see that the Torah teaches us that men should respect their wives. Every story in the Torah is there to teach us something, and this one is no different. During the time period in which Avraham and Sarah lived, the laws were quite different from what we know. When guests would arrive in Egypt, the Pharaoh, or king, would take the women for his pleasure. However, if the woman was married, they would kill her husband so she would be untethered. When this founding couple of our nation went down to Egypt, Avraham asked Sarah if she would please tell Pharaoh that she was his sister so he would not be killed. It would seem that in effect, by doing this, Avraham put Sarah in harm's way, as now she would be free for the taking. However, the *Zohar* explains that Avraham knew that Sarah's merits would protect her, but he was not so sure of his own merits. This is because Avraham respected Sarah and recognized her inner strength (her "circle"). He even relied on it in his time of need, all while asking for her consent.

We see from this story that the Torah clearly shows us how a man should treat his wife: with respect, asking consent, and appreciating her strength and gifts.

We can agree that this was not the norm in those times. The mere fact that the king could just take any woman he desired points to that. So why were women treated so disrespectfully? The answer takes us back to the first sin, an answer we may not like to hear. It took me a while to understand this, but in the end, the idea resonated with me.

During the sin in the Garden of Eden, Chavah let herself be seduced by the snake and, in turn, used her sexuality to convince Adam to eat from the tree. Therefore, since she used her seductive powers to influence her husband to sin rather than using her influence for the good, these powers would now become her detriment. This is the reality until she can repair that sin, namely, by using her powers to influence "her man" to do good. (Interestingly, that is why Esther, who used her powers and influence to convince her husband Achashveirosh to do good, merited to have her son rebuild the Beis Hamikdash. More on that later.[6])

As we women learn and use our influence for good, we regain our initial power in the world. Look around—we can actually see that today!

However, Adam was also responsible. He was seduced by Chavah and sinned; he had no self-control. Therefore, he was destined to work in the fields by the sweat of his brow, with no time for distractions. This is the reality until he can learn to control himself.

As we progress through the generations, we see a definite improvement in the treatment of women in most areas of life. This is due in part to women rectifying the sin of Chavah and in part due to our generation interpreting the deeper, eternal messages in the Torah correctly.

Although at face value, certain Torah sources may seem disrespectful of women, we need to remember that these messages are written in the language of those times; we now need to understand those same sources through the lens of our times. One by one, understood correctly, we will see that they are not barbaric. And their words are not to be taken lightly—coming from a full-blown equalist!

However, as we get further and further removed from the generation that accepted the Torah, the messages are interpreted incorrectly. If we look through the laws and the oral commentary throughout the generations, we see that they stayed with the messages, not necessarily the words. Unfortunately, many like to stay with the text and not take into

---

6    See chapter 9, "Holidays," the section on Purim.

account the evolved oral law, especially in our generation and especially in regard to women. However, that is not what the Torah intended, according to many sources in the Gemara.

What happened to progress? Why does it seem that we are frozen about a hundred years ago? What happened to seemingly stop our evolution as a people?

Well, something traumatic happened. Aggressive assimilation began, and the Jewish nation started losing people in droves, with the youth being drawn to the Enlightenment movement. In Ken Spiro's book *Crash Course in Jewish History*, he delineates clearly how the small insular communities of the Jewish People were broken apart systematically by wars and "enlightened youth." In response, our leaders tightened all the walls in a move to protect the youth.

The Holocaust happened very soon after, and Jewish life as they knew it came to a halt. In terms of halachah, there were nearly no new rulings or applications during this time. It was only afterward that authorities like Rabbi Moshe Feinstein took the leap to make new halachic statements.

A change is happening again if we look around. Women are now part of the Torah discussion, whether through teaching, learning, or writing books (hi!).

For example, in many fully Torah-observant communities, there is a concept of a female advisor called a *yo'etzet*. Working in conjunction with the rabbi, *yo'atzot* can assist women with halachic questions—especially pertaining to *niddah*-related topics that women may be uncomfortable speaking to their rabbi about—and they are accepted by the majority of rabbis. Additionally, many prohibitions traditionally associated with women have simply become obsolete. For example, women can now own property, decide who they will marry, and stand on a stage and speak to crowds of people.

I truly believe that the more we learn over time, the more will be understood in a deeper way—and where necessary, corrected—enabling us to apply our timeless Torah laws within the context of our generation. For example, in many communities, rabbis have figured out a way to make irrelevant a woman's reliance on her husband for the ability to divorce. To this end, the Beth Din of America Prenuptial Agreement, first developed by Rabbi Mordechai Willig, includes a contract stating that the husband will pay his wife a fee for every month he does not produce a *get* once they are living separately. The fee grows each month and is enforceable by the secular court. This gives the husband a clear incentive to give the *get* in a timely fashion, and incredibly, has had a 99 percent success rate. In addition, a more fundamental solution that addresses this difficulty is currently being considered by *rabbanim*.

We need to be patient, keep educating ourselves, and make sure we are fulfilling our individual purpose in this world. We also need to understand that the Torah is not out to get us—quite the contrary. I came across an interesting example of this recently, which drove home this point of the high regard in which the Torah holds women.

When learning about the Torah perspective on women, a problem came up. The Gemara says a seemingly disturbing line about women: "*Ishah kesherah osah ratzon baalah*," which is commonly translated as, "A good wife does the will of her husband."[7]

When I saw this, I was shocked. My immediate reaction was, "Well, who said it?" It was actually said by Eliyahu HaNavi—a great prophet and one of the earliest holders of the tradition. I was astonished. I decided that we must have misunderstood him; there is no way he would say something like that!

I called one of my mentors, and asked her to explain it to me, which she did. While the common translation is "A good wife does the will of her husband," she asked me to translate it word for word in my native Hebrew. I did. The translation came out as "A good woman *creates* the will of her husband."

My mentor explained to me that what Eliyahu HaNavi was saying here was actually an honor to women. He was explaining that a wife creates the will of her husband. She determines the mood of the house, the cravings, the desires. She inspires him, she pushes him—she actually creates what he wills. In a very basic way, she *is* his desire, in

---

7    *Even Ha'ezer* 69:7.

that without her, he would have no desire to be with her and procreate. However, this is only the most basic version. In reality, without the woman, the man's potential is like the arrow with no direction; she creates the will, the direction in which it should go. Again, this does not mean all single men are purposeless and miserable! We all have both energies. Eliyahu HaNavi was merely pointing out how a Jewish woman can be the reason her husband becomes what he does.

This whole experience taught me something. In general, if something seems off or very wrong in the Torah, we probably did not understand it correctly. We might not be the only ones; there might be other men or women understanding it incorrectly as well. However, we are here to grow, not to worry about others' behaviors. We are focusing on ourselves for now. The Torah is Divine. It is holy and perfect. Sometimes it takes a while to understand what it's "getting at"—but it is worth it!

Another small note regarding the two energies and how the female is not "less than" or "subdued."

The Lubavitcher Rebbe teaches that during the final years before the complete redemption, the feminine side of the Creator will shine, and the women in the Jewish nation will be the ones to make the change—just like the women in Egypt were the reason the Jewish nation was redeemed. They did not march around Egypt yelling and protesting. They calmly went about making it happen.

Today, it is our job to make the change in the world needed for Mashiach. It is through our specific energy—calm, wholesome strength—that the world will be redeemed. We should not and cannot let the very wrong definition of calm strength (that we only belong in the kitchen) stop us or define us. We are what the world needs, and we need to step up to the plate.

Like a woman.

I told you I'm an equalist! Can't give up a good empowering moment! But let's get back to our questions, where one last one remains.

There is another concept that comes up often in discussions on feminism.

*Tz'niyus* or modesty.

Now that we know a woman is meant to be the roots, the strong foundation, the calm confidence, we are left wondering what that has to do with our clothes? We also know that modesty laws can be restrictive. Is that to hide us? Why must we cover any areas of our bodies, and what exactly are those areas we must cover? What does that have to do with being calm?

Let's talk about modesty.

CHAPTER 6

# MODESTY

What is modesty? *Tz'niyus*? I know that there are laws with inches and measurements, but what is the actual source or the actual commandment in the Torah?

When I started looking into Jewish modesty laws, I was directed to a book called *The Book of the Women and her Mitzvos* (loose translation of the title) written by Rabbi E.J. Allinson. Since this book is so often quoted in my world as a source for basic halachah, I figured he probably has a source in the Torah for *tz'niyus*. He does.

In the *Navi Michah* there is a *pasuk*: "*Hatzne'a leches im Elokecha*—Go privately [i.e., modestly] with your God."[1] What does this mean? Most of the commentaries on this *pasuk* have the same explanation: Our relationship with our Creator is a private one. God does not need other humans to validate our personal relationship with Him. He doesn't need the whole world to know about it. The Creator just wants us to have that relationship—whether in our souls, in private, or in public—to always be there.

But this does not tell me to be modest, so I kept reading.

I found another source in *Devarim*: "*Al tiskarev l'davar ervah*—Don't go close to something private."[2] However, according to the sources there and the book we are referencing, this is a man's commandment and not really relevant to women at all. It refers to how a man should relate to women while praying or studying Torah.

---

1    *Michah* 6:8.
2    *Devarim* 23:18.

However, the next *pasuk* caught my eye: "*Lo tiheyeh kedeshah m'bnos Yisrael l'zenus.*"[3] Now this was interesting, what does it mean? Says *Rashi*: Do not set yourself aside to be promiscuous. So, there we have it, here is a source! Do not do something that sets you aside in a promiscuous category.

Coincidentally (or not) I was reading this in the Gutnick Chumash, and there was an excerpt from the Lubavitcher Rebbe stating that the way a woman dresses (promiscuous or not) directly affects her children and how they will behave when they grow up. He quoted a source in *Yoma*, where the Gemara tells a story about a woman named Kimchis who had all seven of her sons serve as Kohen Gadol (High Priest in the Beis Hamikdash). When the rabbis asked her what she did to deserve this, she responded that the walls of her home never saw the hairs on her head. The rabbis discuss this in the Gemara, saying that there were many women who did this and none of them merited what she did. They add to say that all of her sons actually died, and therefore a woman should be careful before taking on extreme stringencies. The Gemara concludes by quoting a source in *Tehillim*: "*Kol kevudah bas melech penimah,*" meaning that a woman who internalizes this message will merit great things."

Well, that jumped. First off, the translation is incorrect. In addition, What is this source? And how did it come up here?

Looking at it inside *Tehillim*, I read the commentaries written there. What King David meant by saying that a princess's honor is on the inside was that when a king's daughter walks around in public, she is regal and royal, her clothing distinguished and beautiful. However, when she is alone in her room, not dressed in beautiful clothes—or even beautiful pajamas—she still behaves regally.

In other words, it is not being in public that makes her regal and beautiful; it's what is inside her that counts—which is why she is still regal when she is alone. King David, and the commentaries learning

---

3    Ibid., 23:28.

this source, were explaining the status of a Jewish woman: she behaves regally whether in front of a thousand people or alone with God.

This brings us back to our original source, from which we learned that our relationship with God is not for others; it is between us and God alone. For no matter where we are or who we are with, we are princesses of God and must act accordingly.

To sum up the actual mitzvah of *tz'niyus*, we end up with a positive commandment and a negative commandment:

- The positive is to be regal and beautiful, a princess of God.
- The negative is to not be promiscuous or associated with promiscuous people.

I would venture to say that the difference here lies in the line between beautiful and provocative. This is a very personal mitzvah. A woman should be conscious of being respectful, beautiful, and dignified in the way she dresses and in the way she carries herself.

Still, it is not all subjective. The Torah gives us basic guidelines for what is considered appropriate and what is not. These guidelines are incredibly basic, because the real boundaries are set by the society in which we live. However, the Creator gave some parameters, no matter the moral situation of our society.

Let's break it down topic by topic.

HAIR COVERINGS FOR WOMEN

As we stated in one of the first chapters of this book, every mitzvah we do must have a source in the Torah and be expounded on by our Sages, until it is brought into our generation. So, what is the source for covering our hair? Turns out there are two, and they are completely separate, so let's deal with them one at a time.

Let's go on a tangent here to remind ourselves of how the halachic process works, and what *das Yehudis* is. We start with the *pasuk* in the Torah, find the explanation in the Mishnah, and see what the Gemara teaches about that Mishnah. Then we check if the *Mishneh Torah*, *Shulchan Aruch*, or *Mishnah Berurah* have anything to say, and from there we go into *das Yehudis*, i.e., what our community and society does.

Let's continue on the tangent for one more minute. What is our community and society? When we grow into ourselves, as mentioned above, we need to find the community that applies the tradition in a way that is meaningful for us.[4] The ideal is for us to live in a place that has a synagogue of like-minded people, a rabbi who guides the community and exemplifies how to live according to its guidelines, and a group of people who live around us who feel the same. We need to belong somewhere. Once we have found our place, we can look around and see what the role models in that particular group of people are doing. This is *das Yehudis*, which translates as halachah for the women in that community.

Now, you can't always find a community that has a synagogue and a rabbi and a group of people who feel the same as you. Sometimes life takes us to communities that are not ideal. When that is the case, we need to seek role models that we align with. How are they living their life? Then we compare our observations to the way the role models in our community are living their life. What we end up with is a hybrid, upholding our values but not sticking out in a negative way in the community we live in.

So now that we know what community is, let's learn about hair covering.

What is the source in the Torah? In *Sefer Bamidbar* in the parashah of *sotah*, the Torah explains what happens when a man suspects his wife of committing adultery.[5] Once he has asked her not to be alone with a certain man, and she was later seen by two reputable witnesses going somewhere alone with that man, the husband can take her to *beis din* (Jewish court). There, the Kohen unties her hair, as to embarrass her, and makes her drink "*sotah* water." If she has committed adultery, it is said that the water will kill her (and the "bad guy" as well). If not, she will live and receive many blessings. We learn from this that untying a woman's hair is an embarrassment for her and takes away from her regal pride; therefore, women keep their hair tied up.

Now this wording is vague, as "tied up" can mean so many things. Let's take a look at how the Oral Torah explains this *pasuk*.

---

4    See chapter 4, "The Rabbi."
5    *Bamidbar* 5:18.

The Mishnah tells us that a woman who goes out with wild hair can be divorced; she loses her *kesubah* rights.[6] In that time period, men were not allowed to divorce their wife without substantial reason, as detailed in the Mishnah and Gemara. Interestingly, one of those significant reasons was going out with wild hair!

Now the Gemara dissects this in *Kesubos 72a*. The rabbis discuss this in detail and come to the conclusion that a married woman must have something in her hair or on her head; they do not specify any details. However, they add that this is not enough if your community dictates something specific. This is where *das Yehudis* comes in.

The *Rambam* in *Mishneh Torah* takes it further and reiterates how important *das Yehudis* is. He goes on to explain in detail why violation of *das Yehudis* is a reason for a woman to lose her *kesubah* rights. The *Rambam* argues that if a woman violates *das Yehudis*, she is not respecting the marriage and the union. When she behaves in an untrustworthy manner according to her community and society, her husband can divorce her since, technically, she is not acting like a married woman. Once she has violated the marriage with her actions, she is no longer entitled to her *kesubah* rights should they get divorced.

This is how the topic is concluded. Every married woman must put something on her head. But what? That differs from community to community and is binding for those living there.

Now let's look at the second reason we cover our hair.

In *Shir Hashirim* we see King Solomon extolling his love's beauty, bringing in her hair as an example: "Your hair is beautiful cascading out of your braids."[7] The Mishnah explains this to mean that a man cannot pray in front of a woman's hair. He cites it among many other items in front of which a man may not pray.

The Gemara talks about this Mishnah as well. The Rabbis explain that the Mishnah was referring to *ervah*, the parts of a woman's body that a man may not pray in front of, and that the loose hair of a married woman is an example of *ervah*. The discussion ends here, but the

---

6    *Kesubos* 7:6.

7    *Shir Hashirim* 4:2.

*Mishneh Torah* goes a little deeper, explaining that hair can have a sexual component to it when it is loose and wild, and therefore one may not pray in front of it.

The *Mishnah Berurah* explains *ervah* a little more clearly, stating that there are two types. There is the *ervah* that is never allowed to be seen, and the one that may not be seen while praying (and he adds "or doing anything of a holy nature"). The *Mishnah Berurah* then goes on to say that if there is something a man is not used to seeing, it becomes *ervah* to him for obvious reasons. For a man, there are two levels of *ervah*: one he should never gaze upon, and one he cannot pray in front of. Hair falls into the second category.

Now, it is important to note that *ervah* is not a woman's mitzvah. It is the man's, and it is his responsibility alone. However, that does not mean that as women we should not be considerate and respectful. It also means that when going into a place of worship, or a *makom kadosh* (holy place), we should definitely cover up our *ervah*.

These two reasons—tying up our hair in the way our community does and covering our hair when we are in a place dedicated to Torah learning or praying—teach us the end result of why and how we cover our hair. All married women must put something in their hair. What that something is varies with each community and each woman must figure that out for herself. Beyond that, when going into a *makom kadosh*, regardless of her community, a woman must cover the majority of her hair and can only show up to a *tefach*, or three fingers' width.[8]

Now, I do want to add one thing. For me, for example, the halachah is that something has to be on my head, and it has to be accepted in my community. For me, wearing a long, gorgeous, loose wig is technically allowed according to halachah. However, I personally feel that this is not in the spirit of the law, since the Torah explicitly says not to have loose wild hair. So, I have taken upon myself the extra step of always wearing something in my wig, so it is not completely loose. I think that is an important note: we have to make sure we feel our soul is satisfied

---

8    According to Rabbi Moshe Feinstein.

as well. Rabbi Anthony Manning once told me, "The most important part of *tz'niyus* is being honest and authentic with ourselves. Make sure not to forget that."

Since *das Yehudis* and societal culture are so important here, and for the rest of this chapter on *tz'niyus*, let's do a quick review on what community is.

Community is the group of people with whom you associate, and whose philosophy and understanding of Judaism and Jewish law you follow.

It is a hybrid of where you live, send your kids to school, and the shul you daven in. It is simply which group of Judaism resonates most with you. In short, it is important to make sure you are not associating yourself with the promiscuous people of your town, as the Torah explicitly says not to. But mostly, it is important to be true to yourself, find your community and rabbi, and follow what you know in your soul to be true.

Once you find your community, you want to act as an appropriate, respectful member within that community. Why? *Das Yehudis*.

*Das Yehudis* means the customs of the Jewish women in your community that have developed the status of halachah. What is not accepted in your community as appropriate (i.e., is promiscuous) becomes binding to those living there.

One of my friends explained this in a way I thought made it very clear. She pointed out that the same thing that is considered valuable in one community can be considered very rude in another. Taking off your shoes when walking into someone's house, for instance: in some countries it would be considered absolutely horrific if you walked into someone's house and took off your shoes, while in another country you would be considered very rude and wrong if you kept your shoes on!

Jewish women are commanded to be respectful, upstanding members of society; therefore, once we choose our community, we have to do what that community deems respectful.

In conclusion, if your community deems wigs to be the most acceptable way to cover your hair and scarves as not respectful, you should wear wigs. On the other hand, if your community deems wigs inappropriate and asks you to wear something that does not resemble hair, you should not wear a wig. If your community wants a wig and a scarf, half a scarf, or only a hat, you need to respect that. It is important to note that if your community has an accepted custom that is below your comfort level, and you would like to be more stringent, you should. For example, my community allows loose, long wigs, but I feel uncomfortable wearing loose hair, so I always put something in my wig.

How you cover your hair depends on your community and on which path your soul aligns with.

## NECKLINES AND COLLARBONES

In the same *parashas sotah* that explains hair covering, we also learn to cover our body. But how? The Gemara asks why the Torah had to say, "the head of the woman" and not "her head," which would have been one word in Hebrew ("*roshah*" versus "*rosh ha'ishah*"). We know that every single letter in the Torah is there to teach us something, and nothing is extra, so why the "extra" word?

The Gemara goes on to explain that the reason the Torah adds the word "woman" is to teach us that we uncover her body as well. The Gemara describes in the example of a *Sotah*, how the *Kohen* would also rip her clothes off and then tie them under her arms above her bosom. The Rabbis question why we do not take off all her clothes if that is what the Torah demands.

Rabbi Yehudah HaNasi was the one who answered. Although the Torah does say to rip off her clothes, Rabbi Yehudah decreed to only rip them, as mentioned above. His explanation was that to uncover more of her would be inappropriate, and lead to lewd thoughts by the Kohanim in the surrounding areas.

From here we get the idea of covering our torso. Even in the case of the *sotah*, that specific *ervah* was too inappropriate to uncover. The exact word used is *libah*, meaning "her heart," so we infer from here that the heart, and similarly the armpits—since that is where the clothes began—need to be covered at all times in public.

So where does the collarbone come in?

It is fairly clear that the collarbone is a boundary on the body to help make sure we do not uncover our *ervah*. We can also say that it is

a *tefach* above the heart, once again ensuring we keep our actual nakedness covered. However, I needed a more substantial source than that for
specifying the collarbone.

In *Berachos*, the rabbis say that even the pinky finger is considered
*ervah* while praying.[9] The *Rosh* argues that this is only for what is generally covered.[10] The *Divrei Chamudos* comments there that if a woman
uncovers something that is generally covered, one cannot pray or learn
as he will be distracted and will not have the proper intentions and
thoughts. This is vague, so he goes on to explain, "In my community,
the women uncover the face, hands, and feet, therefore one can pray in
front of face, hands, or feet. One should do what is customary to do in
their community."

Many took this to mean that we must cover all but our hands, face,
and feet. This is where the boundary of the collarbone came in, including the neck with the face. However, to most, this means that one
should do what is generally accepted in their community and neighborhood, and not uncover something that would be considered irregular
for where she lives and who she associates with.

I would like to take a minute to reiterate what we learned about
*tz'niyus* above. As we mentioned, the end goal of *tz'niyus* is to respect
yourself. It is not to walk around like a person who is trying to elicit promiscuous attention, but to act and dress like a beautiful, regal woman.
It is important to dress beautifully and in a stylish manner that builds
confidence, as walking around looking unkempt is disrespectful to who
you are. The purpose is what we think of ourselves, and the guidelines
are just that—guidelines. They are important, and they must be kept
as the halachos that they are. However, let us keep the end goal in mind
so we do not forget the forest for the trees. When getting dressed, it is
important to think: Am I doing this for beauty or for attention from
men? If you feel that not being careful about your collarbone will attract
male attention, you may not uncover it no matter where you live. Just
make sure at all times that you are being honest with yourself about

9    24a:15.
10   *Berachos* 3:37.

what feels right and what you want to do. If there are many areas in which your honest gut feeling varies extensively from your community, it might be time to look into other communities, as we mentioned earlier. Know the difference and know your community's feelings toward it. The basic halachah is to cover your heart and your underarms, but the actual halachah is to do what your society's standards are, and what you consider to be regal.

## ELBOWS

I searched for a while on this question. There does not seem to be a direct source in the Torah for covering our elbows, other than the general commandment mentioned above to not set ourselves aside for promiscuity.

However, there are a lot of sources in the Gemara quoting community norms of covering elbows. According to these, a woman should cover what the women in her community and surroundings cover, which relates to what we were saying above.

Still, there are two sources that hint to covering the elbows.

- The first was in the parashah of the *sotah*, where the Kohen disrobes the woman and then ties her clothes under her arms so as not to stir up lewd thoughts. Some say we can establish from here that our armpits are considered part of our nakedness, or on a more basic level, our torso starting from our underarms. We have to make sure that our armpits are covered even when we raise our arms, and therefore our sleeves need to be long enough to always cover the entire underarm.
- The other hint I discovered referred to pants. The Gemara quotes the *Navi* saying that revealing our *shok* (thigh) is *ervah*. There are a few opinions that state that the upper arm may also be called a *shok*, since we understand *shok* as thigh from an animal, and an animal has four thighs. Therefore, it is possible that our arms are considered the front legs of the animal.

All this considered, if we find the basic commandment in Tanach and then expand on that with our (and our rabbis') understanding, together with community norms, we understand what we need to cover.

For me personally, I interpreted this to mean that my armpit should be covered at all times, even when my arm is raised. This is taking into consideration the understanding of rabbis, my own feeling of what's right, and what the community I associate with does. However, every person has to act according to what the sum of all the factors means to her. I am just bringing this as an example.

There are many communities that hold that the sleeve has to reach the elbow (because of the *shok* concept), and there are also those who say the whole arm is *shok*, and the sleeve must therefore reach the wrist. Then there are those who say just the upper arm must be covered, not the elbow. Again, you need to take a look at the norm in your community.

KNEES

As we said, the Gemara tells us that a *shok* in a woman is nakedness, meaning something that must be covered whenever she is with others. This concept is from the *pasuk* in *Yeshayahu* that speaks about what exile will be like.[11] The *Navi* talks about the women who will have to cross rivers for their masters, and their *shok* will be exposed. Many of the commentaries interpret this as the upper half of the leg; we know from the different parts of the animal discussed in relation to *korbanos* (sacrifices) that the word "*shok*" is used to describe the limb from the hip joint to the knee joint. From here comes the idea that we must cover ourselves to our knees.

There are many who understand this to mean *until* our knees. There are many others who understand this to mean *including* our knees. There are still others who understand this to mean our calves. Once again, you must act based on a combination of your spiritual approach and your community norms.

I heard an amazing story from a person close to me. She told me that a friend of hers needed to have her thigh bone replaced and was being

11   47:2.

prepped for surgery. The surgeon came in to talk to her and to let her know what would happen during the operation. He then showed her a thigh bone and said, "This is what we will be putting in your leg." However, she noticed that the thigh bone had a knee attached, so she asked him why, as she did not need a knee replacement. The surgeon explained that this was not the knee; it was the kneecap, as the kneecap is part of the thigh bone and is all one piece. The woman literally sat up and made him repeat himself. For the first time, she had full clarity of what a thigh really is. To me this is an incredible story demonstrating exactly what is meant in halachah by the word "*shok*."

However, not everyone holds this way, and this is where socks come in. The idea that the *shok* might mean up to the calf and therefore women must cover until their calves would explain why many communities insist on tights—or at least socks. This brought up a question for me. Why are we allowed to wear socks? If we cannot wear pants as they show the shape of the leg, wouldn't socks (or tights) have the same issue below the knee? And if not, can women wear pants?

The obvious answer to the pants question is *k'li gever*, the commandment that a woman should not wear men's clothes (and vice versa). This comes from a *pasuk* in *Devarim* that describes doing so as a *to'evah* (abomination).[12] Today, however, there are obvious differences between men's pants and women's pants; the average man would not wear women's pants, so they would no longer be considered only men's clothing. On a technical halachic level, this view is actually supported by the majority of rabbis.

However, *wearing* pants is not accepted in the majority of communities, and as we must keep to *das Yehudis*, we are required to not draw inappropriate attention to ourselves. If all the women are wearing skirts and I am wearing pants, I will be drawing (promiscuous) attention to myself. However, community norms usually have some kind of source from which they are derived. What is the source here? Why is showing the shape of the leg okay, but only until a certain point?

---

12    22:5.

In *Sefer Yechezkel*, an interesting narrative takes place. God is talking to Jerusalem (or, more likely, the people in Jerusalem) and admonishing them. The *navi* says, "You were abandoned and no one took compassion on you...but I clothed you and bathed you and adorned you with gold and silver...but you became confident in your beauty and you sinned with all that I gave you..." The *navi* goes on to describe the different sins and then arrives at the one that is most relevant to this discussion. He says, "You sat on the street corners and sullied your beauty, you spread your legs and multiplied your promiscuity."[13] The word used for promiscuity, "*taznuseich*," is the same word used when the Torah commands us to be modest: "*Lo tihiyeh kedeshah l'zenus*." If we know we are supposed to refrain from anything to do with *zenus* and that the Torah defines spreading our legs as *zenus*, we learn from here that we should not spread our legs.

The Gemara derives from this that showing the space where our legs separate is not allowed. When we show the shape of our legs all the way up to where they meet, we are separating our legs, which is something the Torah prohibits. According to most opinions, this is considered *ervah*. While all other *ervah* areas of our body can be covered while showing shape, this specific one cannot since the *ervah* is of slightly different components. It is not only the actual part of our body that is *ervah*; it is the shape—the separation itself—that is *ervah*.

From this source we learn that pants are prohibited for women. Showing the area where our legs split is showing the area of promiscuity, and is in effect spreading our legs.

When this is coupled with the other source, stipulating that the *shok*, the thigh, is *ervah*, we get to the final halachah according to most opinions. Most communities feel we have to cover the upper leg so as not to show the separation of our legs. Once again, check what your community does.

---

13   16:25–26.

Let's get back to the basics: There are many different aspects of modesty:

- The explicit message in the Torah
- Mindset
- Community norms
- Personal sensitivity and intuition

We have the basic mitzvah to focus on beauty and royalty and make sure to move away from attracting inappropriate attention. We have to make sure we are always aware of why we dress the way we dress, and we must remember that this is between us and God and has nothing to do with other people.

This is a little bit complicated because on the one hand, we know that *tz'niyus* is an inner trait, a personal sensitivity, and is between me and my Creator, while on the other hand, we know that where we live and who we associate with strongly dictates what is considered appropriate and what is not.

I think that once we have established what is considered acceptable as the societal norm in our community, we can then turn off that part and focus completely on our intuition. If we know for certain that what we are wearing is halachically acceptable, and we know we are wearing it to beautify God's world—not to be promiscuous—then we're good to go.

However, it is important not to go overboard with this. Some women have a tendency to become overly conscious of what they are covering or not. This can lead to body-image problems, shame, and the feeling that our body is in some way bad. There is nothing shameful about our body. It is absolutely beautiful. It was made by the Creator! Some parts are meant to be kept private, but there is nothing shameful about them—only intimate.

I know that sometimes it feels like in order to be modest, we must try to hide, make ourselves unattractive, or be as unnoticeable as possible. However, this is a misconception. As we learned here, the point of *tz'niyus* is not to hide or be ugly. It is to represent God and be a princess. Keep that in mind.

It sounds so cliché and I hate saying it, but it's true: You are a Jewish princess, and that comes with a responsibility to represent God in a beautiful way. You should not walk around looking provocative, but at the same time you should not walk around looking neglected.

You are a beautiful and regal princess. Believe it!

CHAPTER 7

# PRAYER

At this point in my journey, I was in a strange place. I mean, I knew that the Creator created the world, that He loves me, and that the Torah is His guide for how to live the most fulfilling life. I even understood where I stood in it as a woman. But then a new problem came up. I found myself unable to concentrate when praying.

If we believe that the Creator only wants good for us, only wants to give us good, and only will unless we mess that up ourselves, why pray for things to change? Why pray at all? If He made us, He knows what we're thinking—so why pray? And if He only does what's best for us, why ask for something else?

We definitely have a basis for prayer in our history. During the days of Creation, the Torah tells us that nothing had actually sprouted yet, since there was no rain. The Torah goes on to explain that there was no rain since Adam was not there to work the land. But Adam did not work the land until after he sinned, so how could he have been expected to work the land before he was even created? *Rashi* explains that it is "*avodah she'ba'lev*—the work of the heart." The world was waiting for Adam's prayers to bring out its potential. The world was literally all potential until there was prayer. That must mean something.

In addition to that source, we also know that our forefathers and foremothers prayed, and that women and men have prayed throughout history. Everywhere you look in the history of the Jewish People, people prayed.

So, we know that there is definitely something valid about it. But what is the point?

Rebbe Nachman talks about this a lot in his teachings, particularly in his book *Histapchus Hanefesh*.[1] One of the lessons that really spoke to me was the idea that we are not praying as an act of request. When we pray, we are strengthening the relationship between ourselves and our Creator. It is not so much praying as it is connecting. Actively connecting ourselves to our Creator creates a connection through which good things can come to us. It is like connecting two pipes so the water can flow.

But it can go even further than that. Yes, we can connect to the Creator in order to connect the pipes and receive goodness, but what if we connect just for the sake of connection and the receiving is a by-product?

Let me explain what I mean with an example of a child and his parents. When a child has a typical connection to his parents, the child does not need to ask for almost anything. The parents know what he needs and give it to him, but that is only a side point. The special part—the main part—is their relationship.

When the child is sad, when the child had a bad day, where does he go? To his parents! He doesn't necessarily ask his parents to make the pain go away; he simply finds comfort in their embrace and ability to share his woes. If the parent can, they will help the situation—but that is not the main reason the child turns to them.

The same goes for the Creator. He created us, cares for us, and loves us, as mentioned and demonstrated throughout this book. When we talk to Him every day, build a connection, and enjoy His presence, we are strengthening our relationship with Him. What could be better? In the same vein, when we are sad, we don't necessarily have to ask for the Creator to change the circumstances; we can simply find comfort in His presence and in the knowledge that He knows what is best for us.

This does not mean we cannot or do not ask for anything. Just like a child can ask for ice cream, we can ask as well. But this is not the point of the relationship. We can tell Him that a challenge is too big, or we can ask Him to please make it smaller. We can also ask for strength to

---

1    14:3.

overcome, or we can plead for an easier, slower lesson. However, that is not the point of our relationship, and it is not necessarily always what is best for us.

Let us focus on connecting to the Creator for the sake of the relationship, for the sake of love.

Once we start thinking of prayer as talking and connecting, it is easier to talk to the Creator. We can talk to Him all day, in our own words, about anything we want! Every time we do, we are strengthening the connection, the pipe that goes from the Creator to us. By virtue of that, all of His good can flow down to us.

Why then, do we pray when we go through something challenging? Pray for change, strength, or healing? This is when we are asking the Creator for something based on the connection we have built. Once we have built up that connection to the Creator and strengthened it every day, when we need something, it is "easier" for us to get it. Now, that is not to say that if you never prayed before, the Creator will not listen when you finally do decide to pray. Of course, He will. However, to bring a constant flow of blessing and goodness into our lives, we must keep up the conversation and keep that pipe strongly attached to our Creator. We need to keep the connection.

But what about praying for change? If something happens to us, and we believe that everything the Creator does is for the best, then why pray for it to change?

One answer lies in the subject of our prayer. When we are praying for something to stop, we are saying, "This is hard for me. Even though I know it might ultimately be good for me, it's too hard to handle. Please, can You get me to where I need to be in some other way?" Or you can ask for strength. "Yes, I understand that for some reason this is good for me. Please help me see that, because I'm having a hard time with it right now." We are not necessarily complaining or claiming that what God did was not good. Rather, we are asking for strength, or for a different and easier path.

Never, ever think, "I won't pray; it's not worth it," or "Praying for change is not ideal; I just need to accept things as they are." Prayer is always worth it; it builds that connection and it builds you up. We should always talk to our Creator. Always. It should never be thought of as a weakness; in fact, praying takes strength.

In addition, in *Midrash Rabbah*, when discussing Sarah's barrenness, the question is asked: "Why are the matriarchs barren?"[2] Rabbi Levi answers: Because the Creator yearned for their prayers. This is brought from a source in *Shir Hashirim*, "My dove...let me see your face; let me hear your voice."[3] The Creator yearns for our prayers and will sometimes give us nudges to remind us to pray. Since those nudges are there for the purpose of reminding us to nurture the relationship, as soon as we pray, we change the circumstances.

Barrenness is, of course, an extremely difficult challenge, so this may seem harsh. However, we cannot understand the workings of Heaven and we know the matriarchs were on a completely different level spiritually. We receive circumstances on our own level—just enough to remind us, but not enough to crush us, hopefully.

At the end of the day, these nudges are for us because prayer is meant to help us. We nurture our relationship with our Creator to help us feel fulfilled and to open up the channels of goodness. When the Creator wants to give to us, but we close the pathways of communication, He reminds us—gently or not so gently—depending on what we need.

In addition, there are sources in the Gemara that show how prayer can affect what happens in this world. Just like the example of the projector we spoke about previously, we can affect what comes down by what we send up. The Gemara in *Berachos* discusses how prayer can sweeten rulings, rip up harsh decrees, and change fate. Prayer is incredibly important, no matter how we go about it.

So go have a conversation. I get that. But what about the three daily prayers that men are mandated to pray? If prayer is about having a conversation, then how is it helpful for us to have a script and a timetable? In addition, are women mandated in the three prayers? And if not, why?

---

2    45:7.

3    2:14.

The *Maharal*, a scholar and leader who lived in the 1600s, presents a nice idea that explains why prayer is not mandated for women, and why they do not lead prayers for those to whom it is mandated.

He points out that prayer is something that is not always intuitive to man. Sometimes we don't know what to say, how to start, or where to go. For that reason, we have the scripted prayers that tell us what to say, and we have the mandated prayers that tell us when to say it. This way, we never forget or push them off, which would thereby risk our connection to our Creator. Prayer can be like a date night. We should always be talking and maintaining our relationship—but sometimes we need scheduled meetings to do that.

The three daily prayers are not random concepts that the Sages came up with as a substitute for regular conversation. Each was originally formulated, respectively, by our forefathers, and each has many spiritual and mystical purposes and influence. We say the same prayers that Avraham, Yitzchak, and Yaakov said in their conversations with our Creator. That is incredibly special, and connects us to our heritage as well as the Creator.

So why then are women not mandated to pray? Why do we seem to be essentially removed from one of the forms of prayer?

Women do not have to pray the scripted prayers because women intuitively know how to talk to their Creator. Being a mother, or having the ability to be a mother, gives you more of the "Creator" aspect inside of you. This makes the actual Creator feel a little closer and gives you an extra connection so that you can speak freely. And once a woman has children, there is no expectation of her to pray at all. Since she has now become a partner in creation, she has another level of connection with the Creator. It is much easier for her to pray by just having conversations with her Creator sprinkled throughout the day while doing mundane tasks.

Let's take it a step further. Women do not need to pray in the synagogue with other women, but men are expected to pray in groups of ten. Why is this? Because women are innately capable of being connected even when they are countries apart. It is on the tip of our tongues to pray for our friends; we feel our friends' pain, and we are naturally more compassionate. While men are required to be in the same room to pray as a group, women need only to be together in their hearts to be able to pray as a group. We are wired with love and empathy, and this makes us naturally more able to connect.

This does not mean that a woman or mother should *not* pray the scripted prayers or pray in a synagogue. Whenever possible, it is of value, and always will be. However, if she cannot, she is not necessarily missing out, for she has been given the gift of being able to talk to her Creator whenever she wants, as a daughter to a loving father.

We have the three mandated prayers, and we have intimate, conversational prayer. There is also prayer in the form of blessings.

We say blessings over what we eat, after we eat, and over an assortment of other experiences in life. What are these blessings for?

This is where we show gratitude. To go back to the couple analogy, when your spouse takes out the garbage, you don't need a whole scheduled date in response—a simple "thank you" is enough. This is the purpose of a berachah (blessing). It is a simple way to say thank you to the Creator for what He gives us.

Yes, we have conversations and spontaneous prayers. Then we have the mandated prayers, almost like a set date night, to make sure nothing falls through the cracks and to give us a framework. In addition to this we have the blessings we say throughout the day—short sentences that are just the required "thank you," when we take a moment to be grateful for what we have. It is important to be mindful of where everything comes from and to thank the Source, and to not take anything for granted. Once we start taking what we have for granted, we start to lose our connection with our Source. Even in a relationship, when one partner does not appreciate the other, distance grows. It is important to say thank you to our Creator—and to others in our life.

In fact, perhaps prayer can actually teach us how to communicate with those around us.

I feel connected to prayer. It feels seamless, and it makes sense to me. I like connecting to my Creator and having multiple venues to do that. However, I still felt confused by one aspect of prayer: *Tehillim*, the psalms written by King David.

Everyone always talks about how powerful *Tehillim* is, and that you should say *Tehillim* when someone is sick or if you need help with something, etc. But if prayer is for the sake of a relationship, where does *Tehillim* come in?

Rabbi Shimon Bar Yochai, the author of the *Zohar*, the biggest Kabbalist of our nation, says as follows, "Come see how these songs and praises that David recited contain secrets and sublime concepts involving mysteries of wisdom, because they were all recited with *ruach hakodesh*."[4]

The words of *Tehillim* were written with Divine direction from God. They have power as they contain the secrets of creation within them. While we may not always understand exactly what we are saying, the power of the words is huge. King David went through a lot in his life, and this shows in *Tehillim*. The verses vary in mood and are written during various parts of his life. When a person is going through any kind of trouble or pain in this world, they can usually find a chapter of *Tehillim* they can relate to, which opens their souls directly to prayer. There is something mystical in these words—something that should be utilized.

As we learned above, while the Creator knows what is best for us and will push us to our ultimate goal, He also yearns for our prayers, and sometimes asks for them through the "nudges" we mentioned above, which push us to look up and acknowledge Him. During those times, our words of *Tehillim* can direct our prayers when we don't know what words to say. However, it goes deeper than that. Our Creator knows what is best for us and how we can reach our full potential. But sometimes the path is just too hard. It is too scary; we can't see in front of us, and we need help. When we say the words of *Tehillim*, the destination doesn't change—but the path does. It might get illuminated; it might get a little wider. Either way, it becomes bearable through the words of *Tehillim*, especially when we are at a loss of what to say.

Something happened to me recently that brought this point home. When the COVID virus called for more restrictions during the second

---

4   *Zohar, Parashas Vayikra.*

wave, our schools mandated that all children, even young ones, needed to be masked. I was upset and scared about how it would affect my child's social development. If he could not see facial expressions, how would he learn social cues? Add to this the fear of helplessness of what was happening, and I was not in a good place.

The new mandate came out on a Friday afternoon. I got an email that my three-year-old would need to wear a mask all day starting Monday. On Shabbos morning, my neighbor made a little get-together in her house for the younger girls of the neighborhood, and I took my daughter. My neighbor sat all the girls down and explained to them that God listens to the prayers of children faster than those of adults. Since they are children, there are special "express" angels that bring their prayers straight to the Creator, and He listens to them with extra care. She went on to explain that just like Mordechai gathered the children to learn Torah and then began the downfall of Haman, we are gathering the children to pray to begin the downfall of COVID.

It was a sweet talk. The girls said the whole *Sefer Tehillim* together and then we went to shul. On the way my daughter casually mentioned, "Everything is going to start getting better now because the little girls davened; don't worry."

Shabbos was beautiful. After it was over, I turned on my phone to discover that over Shabbos, they had decided to remove the need for masks for young children and let them have a normal school routine, as it is imperative to their development.

It was a moment of clarity. Yes, the Creator knows what is best for us. Yes, prayer is for building relationships and talking and quality time. But we are allowed to ask for help—we are allowed to say this is too hard.

And the words of *Tehillim* are perfect for that. They were written with *ruach hakodesh*. The *Zohar*, and many others, discusses the special power hidden in the words. Rabbi Fine brings Rav Yosef Chayon, who wrote that "King David composed the Book of *Tehillim* because of his great spiritual level and *ruach hakodesh*, as it says "The words of David…who was established on high…"[5]

---

5    *Shmuel II* 23:1.

So next time we feel lost, or scared, or any kind of emotion at all, we can ask for help. We can ask for the path to get a little easier, even if the destination stays the same.

## CHAPTER 8

# SHABBOS

When my baby was still a newborn, Shabbos was almost impossible. I wasn't back to myself at all. My husband was the rabbi of a shul that demanded nearly all his time on Shabbos. On the long summer *Shabbosim*, I didn't know what to do with myself to stop my brain from being overrun with anxiety—or worse. In my weak mental and physical state, I could neither handle all the restrictions of Shabbos, nor care about remembering them. I had to do whatever I could to simply survive each day. I was barely hanging on, and those months were simply traumatic.

Fast-forward a few years: I had found my peace and found my happiness. I was settled with my kids and had learned how to be a really good mom. I was even far into my journey with this book. Unbeknownst to anyone, though, I still didn't quite get Shabbos, and that was affecting me in ways I didn't feel good about. I decided to look into it and start from the beginning.

As usual, we start every question by looking for the source. What is the source for Shabbos? In *Parashas Ki Sisa*, the verse says: "Keep my Sabbaths...it is a sign...that I, God, make you holy."[1]

In this source, the Creator tells us to keep Shabbos as a sign. It even tells us that this sign shows that we are holy. But what exactly is Shabbos?

In *Parashas Yisro* it says, "In six days God made the heavens and the earth...and He rested on the seventh day..."[2] We know that Shabbos means to rest. We are commanded to rest as a sign that we are holy, and we are told that God Himself rested on Shabbos as well.

---

1   *Shemos* 31:13.
2   Ibid., 20:10.

104

This doesn't seem to make much sense. God does not need to rest. He was not tired. He was not overworked. As a matter of fact, the world kept existing, which means that based on what we learned in our earlier explanation of Creation as an ongoing phenomenon, He was not actually "resting."

Rabbi Avrohom Tzvi Kluger explains this in his book about Shabbos, *My Sole Desire*. There are different kinds of rest, and this one in particular is described with the Hebrew word *menuchah*, which is similar to tranquility. In fact, the term in Hebrew for a healthy mental state is *menuchas ha'nefesh*. *Menuchah* is a kind of confident contentment—a calmness without the pressure to accomplish. This calm, restful state is the gift of Shabbos that God gave us.

What exactly is this state? How do we achieve it or even understand it?

Rabbi Kluger explains that *menuchah* is the rest you get when enjoying the fruits of your labor. Just like when you are working on a project, say setting up your daughter's nursery. You work on it and work on it, tweak here, fix there. When the room is complete you sit back and look at it. You say with satisfaction, "This is where she will sleep. This is the room she will live in, and enjoy. I created this, and I am satisfied, now I can enjoy it." You enjoy the calm and beauty of the room, you enjoy your handiwork, and the satisfaction of a job well done.

The same goes for God. The Torah was not telling us that He slept on the seventh day; rather, that He enjoyed His creation. He sat back and admired His work, so to speak. He created the world and all that is in it, and then He gifted it to us. Likewise, He gave us the opportunity to work all week toward our goals, whatever they may be. But then, one day a week we should sit back and enjoy what we have created. In all areas of our life, we stop and enjoy for twenty-four hours. Be it the achievement of spiritual, physical, or emotional goals—or even a small goal that may not seem so significant.

That is why on Shabbos we sit back and enjoy the fruits of our labor. We spend time with our kids and just enjoy them. We enjoy our house, which is why we clean it before Shabbos—so we won't feel the urgency to clean it on Shabbos, and we can just appreciate our home. We don't make money; we enjoy the money we have already made.

The point is that on Shabbos we enjoy what we have accomplished without accomplishing.

This sounds wonderful, but something still bothered me. I understood that God sat back and appreciated His creation; it was perfect and complete. But why command us to do the same? Why did He gift this moment of peace that He had to us? We aren't done on Shabbos; we simply pause. Even more, it is considered a sin for a non-Jew to keep Shabbos. That doesn't seem to make sense.

First, let us answer why God gave this gift to Jews. As we spoke about earlier in this book, the final *Sefirah* of the ten attributes of God is *Malchus* (kingship). Kingship only occurs when the kingdom accepts the leader as their king. It is the last act, the final touch for the world. As the "chosen nation" who accepted the Torah—meaning the kingship—it is our job to bring Godliness into the rest of creation. We take the light and holiness from God and spread it to the rest of humanity, so that they can accept God as their King.

How do we do that if we ourselves are enmeshed in this world? We are not angels who can go from the King to the people; we are just the people. We are the humans who accept God as our King. We are just as enmeshed as the rest of the world; how can we ever spread His light to them?

The answer is Shabbos. For one day a week, God pulls away the curtain and lets us get closer to the King. He reveals the light so that we can bring it to the rest of the world. This is the special feeling we get when we light the Shabbos candles. It is a kind of peaceful energy that enters the home, referred to as the Shabbos Queen. It is our glimpse into the heavens, the secrets of creation. Now is our chance to remember why we are here, and what the point is.

We take a beat, sit back, and enjoy the light. We enjoy what we have accomplished, how far we have come—and then we spread that light. When we stop certain actions, and refrain from distracting ourselves, we make space and focus for this light to be revealed to us.

We have access to this light all through Shabbos. It is strongest during candle lighting, but it is there for the whole twenty-four hours. When we say *Havdalah* (the short ceremony ending Shabbos) we no longer have access to the light as clearly as we did before, but we have the remnants. With those remnants we go into the new week and spread the light of God. We spend Shabbos looking at what we have accomplished and then we spend the week using that to accomplish more, which we then appreciate the following week. When the light runs out, we have another Shabbos for another dose.

This is also why we feel a bit lost after Shabbos is over. That is the curtain closing. Rabbi Kluger says that the *neshamah yeseirah* (the extra soul that is said to be given to us on Shabbos) is not really an extra soul at all. It is the curtain between our body and soul being pulled back so that we can feel more of our soul. When *Havdalah* comes, this curtain is closed and we feel the loss of spirituality.

Interestingly enough, the source for *neshamah yeseirah* is in the Gemara in *Beitzah* where the rabbis discuss the "extra soul" and its ability to eat and drink more (hence the joke that diets don't exist on Shabbos).[3] This sounds kind of funny, so the *Maharsha* explains: It is the ability to elevate food and drink to a spiritual level. This is something we can do all week, but on Shabbos it is easier. Why? Because the curtain is pulled back, more is revealed, and we are holier during these twenty-four hours. Everything we do then is holier. It is not necessarily that we are eating more; just that the act of eating is more elevated.

Another aspect of bringing Godliness into the world is in how we outwardly keep Shabbos. When Jews make it clear that on Shabbos they don't work and are soldiers of God, they remind everyone of their Godliness. When they walk down the streets in their finest clothes to synagogue, everyone knows they are keeping God's Torah. This spreads the light of Shabbos into the world (whether others choose to see it or not). In previous generations, it wasn't easy to work and be observant of Shabbos. If you didn't show up for work on Saturday, you lost your job. Our grandfathers who gave up their jobs every Friday showed the world who the real Boss is. That demonstrates our kingship.

We are not the only ones who keep Shabbos; technically the whole world does. The plants, the animals, the oceans—they all wait for Shabbos as

---

3    16:12.

well. They revel in the light and the feeling of spirituality. We sing about this as Shabbos comes in when we say, "All the trees will sing..."

Actually, before the Creator gave the Torah to the Jewish nation, He asked the other nations if they would like the gift. They were given the option to receive the Torah, and this way they could never claim that had they been asked, they would have accepted. However, they each asked what was written in it, and when hearing one of the commandments, they decided it was too hard and rejected it. But when the Creator came to the Jewish People and offered them the gift, it was only they who answered: "We will do and we will hear." First we will accept, then we will hear what is inside.

This granted us many special privileges, one of which is the gift of Shabbos. Those who are not Jewish could not tap into this energy because they turned away from accepting the responsibility of being God's ambassadors. They are created in God's image, are beloved unto Him, and have a place in the World to Come, but their access to the particular light of Shabbos is closed. Their path to Him is different.

We are privy to be close to the King and see His light once a week, because we chose to make Him our King. We are His ambassadors to the world because we made this pivotal choice.

Shabbos is considered the foundation for all of our beliefs. So much so that according to halachah, if one does not keep Shabbos, he may not read from the Torah because he is not considered a true believer.

Why is this? Aren't there other commandments that would more easily demonstrate our faith? What about prayer? Or Rosh Hashanah? Why Shabbos?

The reason is that Shabbos doesn't make sense. We are commanded to rest. But we are commanded to "rest" in a very particular way, "Rest, but like this, not like that; don't do this or that; and make sure you pray." It gets overwhelming! Most people would say, "If you want me to rest, let me rest the way I want to rest!"

But a true believer knows that at its deepest level, it's not about resting; it's about recharging and reconnecting, and finding spirituality in the day-to-day. And that can only be achieved through disconnecting for a bit, stepping back, and leaning into the spiritual acts of the day.

If a person takes that leap and goes against the logical way to rest in order to keep Shabbos, they are considered a true believer in God. If you let go of all your misconceptions about what relaxing means, or even what appreciation and meditation means, you are taking a leap of faith. You are going against what you believe to be conducive to accomplish the day's goal, and instead doing what God commanded—that is pure faith and proof of faith. You are showing that even when you do not understand, you believe.

This helps us understand the commandments of Shabbos, like dressing in nice clothing, eating festive meals, and praying. These allow us to connect to the spirituality of the day and recharge our souls for the week ahead.

But what do the seemingly stringent restrictions have to do with spirituality?

In order to take pause to appreciate all that we have accomplished and be grateful for what we have been given, we need to unplug from the distractions of the world.

Imagine you are sitting around a bonfire in a camping site with all your favorite people. Sounds amazing right? The warm, crackling fire, the roasted marshmallows, and of course the company. But what if you decided that no one can tell you how to enjoy a bonfire. You are the ultimate lover of bonfires, and nobody can tell you how you should enjoy them. You take away the circle of stones around the fire, you don't clear away the grass, you add sticks way after you should have stopped. What happens? The bonfire becomes a forest fire, and you lose all tranquility.

Less dramatically, Shabbos is like a bonfire. Yes, it is amazing. The company, the food, the calm and relaxation. But now you decide that nobody will tell you how to relax. You take out your phone, you turn on the TV, you decide not to eat three meals. You are now ignoring your family, shutting off your brain, and resting. But now it is just a regular day and the specialness of Shabbos is gone.

In other words, the rules preserve the holiness and specialness of the day. Without them, we would get so distracted, and we would not reach the potential for which the day was intended. Just look around—people who jettison the rules don't benefit from Shabbos. It doesn't work for them.

The Creator knows the secret formula and the reason behind everything. The spiritual acts allow you to enter a holy realm—but the stringencies keep you from falling out. Much like the boundaries of a bonfire protect your fun. The point of Shabbos is not to rest and relax from a hard week. The point of Shabbos is to lean into the spirituality, appreciate what you have, and charge up for the coming week.

Now this does not mean that it is always going to be easy. There are thirty-nine "actions" that one cannot do on Shabbos. That's a lot! Thirty-nine in Hebrew has the same numerical value as the word for dew, *tal* (*lamed tes*). The *Ben Yehoyada* explains that this correlation is to show us that a Jew is obligated to learn about Shabbos and keep the spiritual part correctly, so that the restrictions will feel as light and easy as dew. When they do, you know you have accomplished Shabbos.

As long as the restrictions feel heavy, we will not feel the full impact of Shabbos, because we'll be distracted by what we want to be doing. But once we learn and internalize the spiritual meaning, those same restrictions will feel like nothing, or more accurately, light and refreshing like dew—and that is the true Shabbos feeling. In other words, when we understand the system, it becomes a pleasure to live by it.

In order to do so, we have to make sure we are not turning it into a miserable day of rules and restrictions. When there are so many rules and we want to keep them all, we can sometimes forget about the destination while on the road. Yes, the rules are there to protect the holiness of the day, but if the rules are making the day unholy—full of fighting and anxiety, then we need to zoom out, see how we can keep this mitzvah correctly for our soul, and zoom back in correctly.

In addition, as moms, we sometimes feel like this day is just a long day of kid watching, meal prepping, serving, and cleaning. If that is the case, you need to sit down with your husband and have a serious conversation about how Shabbos can be more conducive for *menuchah* for both of you—and you will both need to compromise on certain things. For example, for me, having quiet time after candle lighting is the crux of Shabbos. In the winter, when my kids are still awake at that time, my husband takes them to shul (yes, even when they were three and four). No, he didn't necessarily get an amazing davening in—but during that time, this was our priority.

There are two aspects to each mitzvah in the Torah: the spiritual (*zachor*) and the physical (*shamor*). "Remember" the gift, which is spiritual, and "keeping" the halachos, which are physical. In doing this we are bringing the spiritual into the physical, which is the exact purpose of Shabbos.

These actions are considered so holy that we even have laws for how to behave on Erev Shabbos, the day before Shabbos. We want to make sure we are protecting the holiness of the day.

For example, the *Kaf Hachaim* explains that one should not go too far from his home on Erev Shabbos so that he has enough time to come back and prepare for Shabbos, and that even those who have servants to prepare the house and food should themselves do some sort of preparation. We see this multiple times in the Gemara:[4]

- Rabbi Abba would go out and purchase the meat for his cooks.
- Rabbi Abahu would sit on a chair and fan the fires cooking the food.
- Rav Safra would roast the head of an animal.
- Rava would salt the fish.
- Rav Puppa would prepare the wicks for the Shabbos candles.

Every single Jew should take part in preparing for Shabbos, as this demonstrates that they are respecting the gift.

The physical acts we do before Shabbos connect us to Shabbos, and the spiritual acts on Shabbos help us connect to its light. Once I started thinking about how my spiritual acts are helping me connect to the holiness of the day, this made me curious. I began wondering how exactly this works. I mean, it's one thing to know that lighting candles connects you spiritually. But what are you supposed to keep in mind when actually performing the act? What happens exactly?

So, I started from the beginning of Shabbos and went all the way through, trying to find an explanation for everything.

---

4    *Shabbos* 119a.

## CANDLE LIGHTING

If the whole point of Shabbos is to bring the spiritual into the physical, then we achieve that by elevating physical items with spirituality. When we take a physical object and do a good deed with it, we infuse that object with holiness from that mitzvah. This brings the holy and spiritual into the mundane, so that the mundane becomes special. It can feel overwhelming to bring the holiness of Shabbos into the week. It sounds nice in theory, but it can feel hard to implement. This is why we do simple mitzvos throughout Shabbos that show us how to infuse the physical with the spiritual.

Lighting the Shabbos candles is the first mitzvah of Shabbos. Fire represents spirituality—passionate and energized. Fire can burn objects and evaporate liquids, turning them into air that rises up to the sky and evaporates. But when we attach that flame to a candle, the fire is instead transformed into something useful. Now instead of only consuming, the fire provides light, warmth, and even ambiance.

Besides for infusing the candle with holiness by uttering the blessing, we demonstrate something else as well. When we attach the spiritual properties of a good deed to something physical, we make that object holy. When we add fire to the candle, we make it useful and long-lasting. So, let's put these two ideas together. Not only do we make the fire substantial; we also take the fleeting physicality and make it useful by infusing it with the holiness of a mitzvah. When we use a candle and fire to do a mitzvah, the result is huge. This is one example of how the whole world can be sanctified with a mitzvah.

This is the moment the curtain is pulled away. This is when the other half of our soul is revealed—the inner, deeper light. This is the exact moment you can feel peace descend on the home, no matter what was happening before.

## KIDDUSH

Why do we make *Kiddush*? Such a seemingly strange ritual over a glass of wine! We already set the day apart by lighting the candles, preparing the house for Shabbos, and praying. Why the need for *Kiddush*?

We spoke about the two sides to Shabbos, *shamor* and *zachor*, to protect and to remember. By setting the day apart, *shomer*, we protect and keep it. By blessing it, we remember its specialness. *Kiddush* is not a strange ritual, rather, it is the exact words written in the Torah from when we were given this special gift. It is our memory of the holiest gift on earth. We make *Kiddush* over wine, as wine is mentioned in multiple places in Jewish sources as an elevated drink for special occasions.

When we say or listen to the words of *Kiddush*, we remind ourselves that we are the chosen nation, we are here to spread light, and we were given a special gift to facilitate that. It's kind of like remembering the words our loved one said when he proposed. We bless the gift, the God Who gave it, and the day.

## THREE MEALS OF SHABBOS

While we're on the topic of meals, I can understand the concept of eating one meal together to appreciate each other and celebrate. But why three? Why not two—or four?

When Moshe told the Jews that they should save half of the double *mahn* that fell on Friday for Shabbos, he used the word "*ha'yom*—the day," three times.[5] Our Sages deduced from this that we should eat three meals on Shabbos. The Jews took the extra *mahn* they received on Friday and divided it into three, so they could eat three meals on Shabbos. But why does this matter so much? Just because Moshe, when speaking of the *mahn*, said "the day" three times, why do we take that to mean three meals? What was so special about the *mahn* that we infuse it into the beginning, middle, and end of Shabbos?

This leads to another question: We start each of the meals on Shabbos with challah, which symbolizes *mahn*. Why is the *mahn* so significant? It was a miracle that lasted only a short while in the scheme of things. Why should it dictate how many meals we should eat on Shabbos, and what we eat with each meal? I can understand that we should sit down to a festive meal to enjoy the fruits of our efforts, namely, being able to afford food due to our work. We also take the time to be with family and

---

5    *Shemos* 16:25.

focus on what is really important. But why the two loaves of challah, braided just so, under a beautiful cloth?

The *Sifsei Chachamim* asks another question. (Yes, I am answering a question with a question, a proud Jew!) Why do we say that Shabbos is a day of blessing when it seems that Friday is? Friday is the day a double portion of *mahn* fell, while on Shabbos none fell. Doesn't it seem that Friday is doubly blessed and Shabbos not at all? However, the *Zohar* explains: Shabbos is *"mekor ha'berachah*—the source of all blessings."* There does not need to be any representation of blessing on this day since the day itself is the blessing and is blessed. The *mahn* only fell in double on Friday because of the blessing of Shabbos. The *Zohar* explains, so too do all the blessings we get during the week come about through the channel of Shabbos.

This ties into what we were saying about Shabbos as the day we sit back and enjoy the fruits of our labor. If we did not have time to enjoy the blessing, we would not know we were blessed! Shabbos is the source of all blessings because it is the moment we realize how truly blessed we are, no matter what we have, and we appreciate it. It is this appreciation and gratefulness that opens the channels to bring more blessing the next week. This is the source of all blessings in our lives!

This reveals another essential point: the importance of gratitude. We know that if someone gives and gives, but the receiver does not show appreciation, resentment will build up and the giver will eventually stop giving. However, if one is grateful and reciprocates in some way, then the giving never ends. In fact, it creates more blessing since now there are two people giving. It is important to be grateful to other people, but it is also important—maybe even more so—to be grateful to God, as this brings more blessing. The Creator knew this and gave us the gift of a day in which we can access that blessing.

Yet a third lesson from the *mahn* is the lesson of faith. On Shabbos we don't work, even though that might go against our instincts. We do not answer any email, no matter how important. Why?

When the Jews were in the desert, the *mahn* was a test of their faith. They had to firmly believe that every morning they would get food, because there was nowhere else for it to come from. If they tried to save *mahn* from the day before, it would rot. The *mahn* taught them to have faith in God that it would fall every morning and double on Friday.

The *mahn* reminds us that we need to be grateful—that despite all our efforts, in the end, everything comes from the Creator. It is a testament to our faith. When the Jews got to Israel and no longer had the *mahn* to remind them of this, they had the bread in the *Mishkan* and the *lechem hapanim* in the Beis Hamikdash. Today, when we no longer have the *Mishkan* to house the bread, we put challah on our tables to remind us, on this day of appreciation, that we also must have faith—and that this is the source of our blessing. Yes, we enjoy the fruits of our labor. However, at the end of the day, everything comes from God.

The *Ben Ish Chai* writes that anything holy is referred to as Shabbos, as it comes from the next world, which is called Shabbos. Anything physical or worldly is called *chol* (weekday), as it pertains to this world. Therefore, says the *Ben Ish Chai*, one should make sure to only speak about Shabbos topics on Shabbos, to stay in that holy realm of spirituality. So much so that even just planning what will be after Shabbos is considered taking away from the specialness of Shabbos. Because when we are exposed to the spiritual realm, to the higher world, why would we need to think about mundane things? The only time this is acceptable is if one talks about the mitzvos he is going to do the following week, because he is thereby planning the spirituality he will bring with him to make it last throughout the week.

Let us make Shabbos our source of light for the week, and let us spread *malchus*, Kingship.

## MELAVEH MALKAH

We learned above that we eat three meals on Shabbos and we learned the reason why. However, there is a fourth quasi-meal called *Melaveh Malkah*. It's an interesting kind of meal as it is not officially part of Shabbos, and takes place on Saturday night after Shabbos is already finished. Why do we have this fourth meal? As usual, we look for the source of the mitzvah, and from there we usually find the meaning as well.

The first time we see mention of the "fourth" meal is in the Gemara where the Rabbis are talking about the three meals we eat on Shabbos.

They explain that one must set the table before and after Shabbos as a way to honor it, as Shabbos should not come to or go from a messy house.[6] This is a hint that there is something we should do to mark the time after Shabbos, but it's not clear yet what. It could be as simple as making sure the table looks nice and clean.

The *Arizal*, one of history's greatest Kabbalists, who lived in Tzefas about 450 years ago, also discusses the idea of *Melaveh Malkah*. He explains that one should refrain from doing weekday work until after one eats *Melaveh Malkah* because the *neshamah yeseirah* is still present.

This does not seem to make much sense since we learned that the *neshamah yeseirah* leaves immediately after Shabbos is over. What is she lingering for? A meal? What is this *Melaveh Malkah* we keep mentioning?

I heard a beautiful explanation by Rabbi Moishe New on TorahAnytime.

He describes how generally in Judaism, the night precedes the day. During Creation, the Creator sets each day by saying, "It was night and it was day, day one." Whenever we celebrate a holiday, it starts at night. However, when the *mahn* fell in the desert, the day preceded the night. The *mahn* would fall every morning, and it would feed the people throughout the day and all through the night. The same was true for the *mahn* that was supplied for Shabbos. Twice as much *mahn* fell on Friday, and this gave enough food for Friday, Friday night, Shabbos, and Motzaei Shabbos (*Melaveh Malkah*). So even though Shabbos was over, and according to Judaism it was technically the next day, they continued eating the food that was blessed with Shabbos.

This is why the *Arizal* says not to work until after *Melaveh Malkah* is finished. Because the soul and blessing of Shabbos is in that meal. We are so lucky to be able to eat from that food!

Just one more way to bring Shabbos into the week.

---

6    *Shabbos* 119b.

# CHAPTER 9

# HOLIDAYS

After talking about Shabbos and how it helps apply everything we learn in theory about spirituality, it got me thinking. Maybe Shabbos helps once a week, but in a bigger way the holidays help throughout the year, each with their own individual message.

I decided to delve into each one over the course of a year as they came, to focus less on cooking, and more about the actual holiday and what its purpose is. This was not part of the book initially, just my own personal way of connecting to each holiday as a proud Jewish woman.

I shared these thoughts with my friends, and they sparked so much thought, application, and conversation that I decided to add them to the book.

So naturally, I'd start with Rosh Hashanah. However, in a way, Rosh Hashanah really starts on Rosh Chodesh Elul, the first day of the preceding month.

ELUL

This month usually generates mixed feelings in our nation. Some people are all for it, shaking and begging and growing closer to their Creator. Others dread it and are filled with anxiety, with no idea how they will make it through. Some ignore the whole month and pretend it's not happening, while others feel nothing at all and pass through the time period obliviously. Strangely though, there are those who dance through it, happy and on a high. I wanted to understand where this last group was coming from, and maybe be like them.

I started looking into what Elul really is about to try and see what the point of it is. I wanted to forget everything I'd learned growing up and start afresh.

The number one lesson we are always taught is that "Elul" is an acronym that stands for "*Ani l'dodi v'dodi li*—I am to my Beloved and my Beloved is to me." We are also always told that the "King is in the field." Which is it? Is my Beloved coming or is the King coming?

It is both. It is the month you receive a Waze notification that your beloved father, whom you have not seen for a year, is coming to visit. Picture the scene. What would you do when you got that notification? You would run to make sure the house is clean and the kids are dressed; you would put a smile on your face, put out cake and tea, and get yourself ready. You would be so excited!

Now add to that the element of awe. Yes, you love him, you are so excited to see him, but you also know that he is an amazing human who has changed the world and done so much for you and others, and you respect him so much.

Wouldn't you be happy? Excited? Wouldn't you feel honored that this amazing man is coming to your home, and feel lucky that you are his daughter, and that he has a special place in his heart for you?

That is on a human level. Now add to this the element of God, and there are no words to explain the feeling.

I saw an amazing story from Rabbi Lazer Brody. Not so much a story, but an explanation on a section of *Navi*.

After the Jews came back from the first exile of seventy years, they gathered in Jerusalem to read the Torah. Imagine: men, women, and children all coming together to listen to the Torah that they had not heard in seventy years. Most barely even spoke Hebrew at this point.

The prophet is standing on a stage built specially for this occasion, and he starts reading. Now, everyone starts crying! They heard all the parts of the Torah that they were supposed to be keeping and realized how far they had strayed, and they started to cry.

But the prophet stops them. He tells them they are not allowed to cry because today is a holiday for God, and we are not allowed to cry on days designated as holidays. How could today be a holiday, they asked. Look how far we've fallen! The prophet answered: Yes, but now you are home. You are on your way back and this is a time to be happy and look forward.

This is Rosh Hashanah, this is Elul—not to dwell on the past but to look forward and be happy at the reunion.

Now, this does not mean the past does not have to be dealt with. Of course, it does. But not right now. Take, for example, a son who leaves his father's home and goes out on the streets to lead a "bad" lifestyle. He is partying, smoking, doing drugs, and many other things he should not. After many years, he knocks on the door of his father's home and says he wants to come home. What is his father's reaction? To hug him! To be so happy he is back! To bring him in and feed him and give him a comfortable bed.

Once he is settled, and they have hugged and enjoyed each other a little bit, then they sit down to talk. They talk about what went wrong, and how to make sure it doesn't happen again. They fix their errors and patch up their relationship and make plans for the future. That is when they talk about the past.

But the first step is the hug. Coming home. And that is Elul.

If Elul is all about rekindling that relationship, how do we do it? To rekindle a relationship takes two parties, but what can I possibly give to my Creator? I can do what He asks, fulfill my potential, and work on myself for the sake of that loving relationship.

This question lingered. While all of this resonated with me and made sense, I still had this thought in the back of mind: Yes, this is all wonderful, but what about the God I grew up with? All-knowing? The One Who punishes, the One Who gets angry? While I was never told straight up that God is angry, I was always taught that there are two components, so to speak. What about "that" side of God—the negative, punishing side? Are we simply going to say it doesn't exist?

Yes, exactly that. God is not vengeful or angry or anything like that. When seen in context, the overall backdrop is extremely different. God is *all* good. We see awe, we see all-powerful, but we do not see vengeful or terrifying. Yes, there is anger, but the anger is mixed with love, and is always forgiving in the end. So where did this idea of a terrifying God come from?

During the time we spent in Europe surrounded by Christianity, the culture of fear and a terrifying God permeated our culture and attached

itself to our teachings. It impacted the Jewish nation since that is
what religion was culturally. However, this is not Judaism. Or Islam,
or present-day Christianity, even. It simply represented the Christian
approach of those days and has no place in our Judaism.

We must remember this, when we catch ourselves thinking in this
way. God does not hate us and never will. God is not scary or terrifying.
He is full of love and goodness. Elul is about coming home; rekindling
our relationship with God by praying and honoring Him. Let us focus
on walking through the door.

ROSH HASHANAH

So now that we know all this, how do we enter Rosh Hashanah? We
understand that He is a loving King, but He is still a powerful King,
Who is deciding all aspects of this year for me. That is terrifying.

I also had another question. I am being taught that my perception of
this "scary king" is wrong, but at the end of the day, everything that
happens during the year is decided on Rosh Hashanah—and bad things
do happen. If He really is not scary and really does love me, why is He
decreeing unpleasant and challenging circumstances for me, on this
day, for the year ahead?

I always go back to the example of parenting and children because it
is one that I relate to and can understand, and I feel is easy to explain
and grasp.

My daughter was diagnosed with celiac at thirteen months. This
means she cannot have gluten, and that at the time of writing this book,
she was labeled with "failure to thrive." She has to eat five meals a day,
which have to consist of four food groups. She cannot eat a lot of food
items because she has to stay gluten free, and she also has some oral
muscle issues due to her food trauma.

When I make my daughter sit down and eat food she doesn't like,
when she isn't hungry, she gets really mad at me. When I take my
daughter out of camp or school to take her to doctor appointments,
she gets very upset. She doesn't always understand why I have to take
her to get prodded and tested and make her eat foods she doesn't
want. But that doesn't mean for one second that I don't love her, right?

Au contraire, it is proof that I do! If I wouldn't take her to the doctors and wouldn't make her eat, I'd be neglecting her.

Although to her—with her limited understanding—my actions seem horrible, we all know that it is not only a sign that I don't love her; it's proof that I love her so much.

The same goes for our Creator. We do not always understand the point of what is happening, but this does not mean for one second that it's not for our best.

We can even take it a step further, as explained to me by a mentor of mine, Manya Lazaroff.

We are in this world to become the absolute best human we can be, and to elevate the world, elevate our soul, and fulfill our purpose. Now, if we stray from that path and start heading in a direction that will not help us achieve our goal, the Creator ever so gently places us back on that path.

Now, we do not always perceive it as gentle. As a matter of fact, we can sometimes feel it as downright abusive. But it is always in just the right measure, and that is where faith comes in. As we mentioned above, we can always ask for the challenge to be easier, to take a longer route back to the path that is less thorny. [1] Still, the Creator will do whatever it takes to make sure we are headed in the direction best for our soul, and not straying so far that we cannot achieve our purpose for having come to this world.

Imagine you are on a diet. You hire a personal trainer who is helping you work out and stick to your diet. Would you appreciate it if the trainer turned a blind eye whenever you cheated? What if they let you skip workouts when you weren't in the mood? Maybe they'd make you work out, but they keep it easy so you don't have to work too hard. What do you think? Will you see results? I don't think so.

When we have a goal to meet, we have to work hard to achieve it, and we need support and guidance on the way so we don't get lost. We need someone to be there to help us stretch and sweat and keep away from

---

1    See chapter 7, "Prayer."

the chocolate. The same goes with life itself. If we don't get stretched or break a sweat, we're not growing and accomplishing as much as we can. That's how we know that although it may seem like a "bad" decision has been made for us, it's actually not bad—just stretching.

During these days between Rosh Hashanah and Sukkos, we chant the thirteen attributes of God. As a general rule, the synagogues chant this in a haunting melody that very much induces fear, but this does not seem to match what we spoke about above, or the actual words themselves! In the chant are thirteen descriptions of our Creator—thirteen attributes He described Himself as having. "God of mercy, and kindness, gracious, full of giving, and truth…cleans us of all sin…" Why do we feel scared while we say this? We should be comforted that our Creator is so kind and is sure to forgive us.

An answer that came up a few times in the different places I searched for an answer was as follows: The melody is one of awe, not fear. Not intimidating awe, but rather, an "Oh wow, You are AWEsome!" kind of awe. This is sometimes misunderstood, even by Jews.

Let's look at these thirteen attributes. The first two attributes seem identical; they both consist of the five letters that symbolize God. So actually, it seems that there are only twelve attributes, as the first one is repeated. But the two seemingly identical attributes are intentionally mentioned separately. Why?

We mention the word God twice to imply that God never changes. No matter what we do, no matter how we affect our relationship with our Creator, He Himself never changes. He remains the same both before and after. No matter what we do, His love for us does not change. There is nothing we can do that will change how He feels toward us. Nothing at all. God, God. Constant, unchanging, loyal. The most loving king of all.

In going through the attributes, I came across another one that confused me, *nosei avon*. Technically it means "carrying sins." Now, why would I want my Creator to carry my sins? To hold my sins? Please, just get rid of them! The answer lies in a faulty translation. *Nosei* means "to carry," but in a different way. We have a rule that one action leads to another, and so on, and God created the world in a way where one good deed will lead to another good deed and another. However, in creating this phenomenon of one action leading to the next, the same occurs with sin. One sin leads to another and another, and so on. One of God's attributes is "*Nosei avon*—He carries sin." In other words, God lifts the sin out, stopping the cycle, and prevents us from being led to another sin. This is a symbol of His mercy toward us. Even though we initiated a sequence of events that should lead us to sin, the Creator helps us out and stops it. It seems that the more we learn, the clearer God's love becomes. Amazing.

So, when we stand before God on Rosh Hashanah we have two goals:

- To crown Him as our king and celebrate with Him on this amazing anniversary. We dance and sing and are full of love. We are in awe at His capacity to forgive.
- To ask our Creator to please stretch us in ways that we can perceive as good, and to make it easier for us. (We also focus on this largely on Yom Kippur.) And then we dance, because we know He will—because He loves us.

So, in essence, today's goal is to celebrate our relationship with the Creator, Who is so awesome yet mine.

In the analogy we mentioned above about the boy coming home after being gone and astray for so long, Elul was the hug—and Rosh Hashanah is the meal.

## YOM KIPPUR

Okay, once we've celebrated our relationship, came in for that first hug, and gotten ourselves settled, it's time to sit down and have a talk.

We have done things we are not proud of. We've made mistakes and taken wrong turns that we don't want to remember. Now what? Do we simply promise that we'll do better?

The Chafetz Chaim quotes King David, who says that in order to do good, a person must move away from evil: "*Sur mei'ra v'aseh tov.*"[2] When we tell God, "Okay, I'll do better," we acknowledge that the first step to change is to leave the negative behavior behind. We have to come

---

2   *Tehillim* 34:15.

up with a plan that will help us quit, make the good be something that appeals to us, and go from there.

However, we also have to apologize. We do that on Yom Kippur. We sit with our Father, who also happens to be an amazing King of all kings, and we apologize. We apologize for distancing ourselves, for desecrating His name, for not being as awesome as He created us to be.

Now, from God's perspective, He forgives us.

One proof is my life, and I am sure many others can relate. I mean, I've done plenty of wrong things in my life. I am far from perfect and have made my share of "spiritual bad choices." Yet, my life is pretty good. If God gave me a life according to my sins, I would not be happily married with two beautiful, relatively healthy children and a gorgeous house and an awesome career. That in itself is proof of His forgiveness.

Proof of His love? If we were not loved by the Creator, He would not have given us the Torah. We would have been left to our own devices to figure it all out on our own, and we would not have done very well. We also have a promise. When Moshe came down from Har Sinai and saw the Jews dancing around a golden calf, he broke the *Luchos* containing the Ten Commandments. Then he went back up the mountain and prayed for forty days that God forgive the Jewish People. On day forty, the Creator announced, "I have forgiven them as you asked." This day was Yom Kippur, and the Creator promised to forgive us every year on this day—to enable us to turn to a clean page and start over.

However, forgiveness is not the only thing that happens on Yom Kippur. God is also looking at us and our potential, and how much further we have to go. He is checking to see if we are on the right path or not, and how far from the path we have gone. Based on these findings, the next year is decided. What will have to happen in order to get us back on the path to reaching our goals? While the Creator is deciding this, we stand in the synagogue and pray that those circumstances be ones we can handle, ones we can understand, and ones we can enjoy—not suffer from.

In *Tehillim* 27, the chapter we say every day during this time period, we call God our "light and savior."[3] He lights up the darkest places

---

3   *Tehillim* 27:1.

within us, exposes it all, no matter how bad or scary, and then saves us. This is what takes place on Yom Kippur: a cleansing. Now, does this mean that you can do whatever you want and then say, "I'm sorry," and God will forgive you? Maybe, maybe not. I wanted something deeper than that. I wanted a better relationship. To me, closeness is the goal and forgiveness is just a side benefit. If by sinning I would be harming that closeness, I would try not to sin even if I know it will be forgiven.

It is important to note that the cleansing of Yom Kippur takes place regardless of our awareness of and capabilities on the day. As women, we may not be able to get to shul, and some—for example, after birth—may not even be able to fast. Of course, we need to take the day as seriously as we can, but we need not feel we are missing out if the day is spent at home, taking care of our kids, or otherwise engaged in mundane activities. The same cleansing will happen to us, as long as we each do our best within our personal circumstances. In fact, many sources state that the cleansing is less painful for those who spend Yom Kippur taking care of God's children.

Yom Kippur is a serious day, but it is still full of love and acceptance. We are simply working on a plan for the future so we will grow each year. And then we dance.

## SUKKOS

Now, once the son comes home, embraces his father, and has a serious conversation, it's time for them to enjoy each other. However, Sukkos is kind of strange if you think about it. In Elul, we grow closer to God; on Rosh Hashanah, we crown God as King and celebrate our relationship; and then on Yom Kippur, we get even higher by deepening that relationship, healing the past, and starting a new page. We are on the highest of highs…and then we move into huts. It seems odd.

Even on a bigger scale it seems really strange to celebrate in this way. Sukkos is one of the three major holidays in the Jewish calendar. The first is Pesach, the holiday celebrating the fact that we left Egypt. That's a big deal! The second is Shavuos, celebrating the fact that God gave us the Torah, which we have established is the ultimate gift. We became

His chosen nation! And on the third holiday, we celebrate that we slept in little booths when we left Egypt. Hmm. It doesn't seem to fit.

Not only does Sukkos not seem to be commemorating a big event, it doesn't seem to be commemorating any event at all. While Pesach celebrates the night we left Egypt, and Shavuot celebrates the day we received the Torah, Sukkos seems to celebrate the forty years that we lived in the Clouds of Glory. Is it celebrating any particular event at all?

Let's see what we are really celebrating, since there must be something more that we didn't see at first glance.

There is another place in the Torah where Sukkos comes up. When Yaakov left Lavan's house with his wives, he left Ramses and came to Sukkos. The Torah explains to us that Yaakov named this place Sukkos because he built little huts for his cattle there, and Sukkos means booths. Interestingly enough, the first place the Jews arrived at when they left Egypt was a town called Sukkos. This was a town in which there were many, many huts set up.

The difference between Yaakov and the Jews that left Egypt was who it was that slept in the huts. While Yaakov put his cattle in one hut and the humans in another hut, the Jews leaving Egypt slept together with their cattle in the huts that had already been erected there.

So, picture the scene. The Jews had just left Egypt. They are on this high, but they're also afraid to go into the desert and unsure of what is coming. (Incidentally, four-fifths of them stayed behind in Egypt. One has to be brave to accept and experience Exodus.)

Here are the Jews, in the middle of the desert, sleeping in huts, with their livestock. We can only imagine how they felt; it must not have been too secure. As horrible as Egypt was, they had been living there for over two hundred years and were settled there. I, for one, can understand that they might have been feeling a bit nervous at all the sudden changes, no matter how bad things had been for them.

Yes, they were free. But they were also scared, homeless, and they didn't even have normal bread to eat!

What makes these Jews—our ancestors—so special is that they made the hard choice. They left food and shelter behind to go to the unknown with an invisible God. All just to be free. This is a true act of faith!

Deep in the desert wilderness, it was just man and his God. And God remembers this as a love and kindness from us. He speaks of our actions with tenderness in *Sefer Yirmiyahu*, saying how special it was that we trusted Him so.[4] This was the first moment in which we showed the Creator that we are just as invested in this relationship as He is. It was a moment of solidifying who we were in the process of becoming.

We trusted Him, even sleeping in the desert with our cattle in huts. And in turn, He gave us "huts" made of Clouds of Glory, with all the luxuries we could want.

So Sukkos is not about the forty years we spent living within clouds. Sukkos is about the first night out of Egypt—the night where we slept in huts and said, "We trust God." This was the night we made firm our trust in the Creator and created a mutual relationship with Him. It was an epic moment in the history of the Jewish People and their Creator.

So, in a way, it makes sense for us to celebrate Sukkos after Yom Kippur. We came to our father's house and knocked on the door. We hugged him and celebrated and then had the real conversation about our past. After that, we sat remembering the good times, solidifying the relationship and rebuilding trust.

There is another reason why the holiday of Sukkos falls after Yom Kippur.

If you think about it, it actually makes more sense for Sukkos to be after Pesach. We left Egypt, slept in a hut, and then got the Torah. Why do we not celebrate in that order?

If Sukkos were to be celebrated straight after Pesach, this would be right at the start of the harvest, when abundance is evident before us. The days are warm and getting warmer, the future is bright, and we can see our crops growing. It is not hard to trust when everything seems clear-cut and straightforward. However, we celebrate Sukkos just when it starts to get cold. At this time, things are not so certain, and dark, short, cold days lie ahead. It is here, in the dark and uncertainty, that

---

4    2:2.

we say, "We trust You." That is the ultimate trust, and that is why we celebrate Sukkos when we do.

Sukkos is not just about going outside to commemorate the *ananei ha'kavod* (the clouds of glory). It is about celebrating that first night in a cold hut, with the cattle sleeping next to us. The first time we really trusted our Creator, in the dark. It's the solidification of our relationship.

## CHANUKAH

I was excited to delve into this one. Since moving to the States, I've noticed the general attitude of non-Jews is that Chanukah is just the Jews' way of celebrating "the holidays." However, this bothered me a lot. Chanukah is celebrated with light in the darkest time of the year. You just know something special is going on here. However, there seem to be a lot of similarities between Chanukah and Christmas, with the general timing, tradition of giving gifts, and seasonal lights. We've all heard the stories of the Maccabees and the miracle of the oil that burned for eight nights. But is Chanukah really just a different way to celebrate the winter solstice?

Aside from the fact that Chanukah existed long before Christmas, to me it seems impossible that Chanukah is just a "Jewish Christmas," for the main reason that Chanukah is all about not succumbing to other religions. It's about not giving in, keeping our unique religion alive, and not being influenced to sin.

So why are they so similar?

Academics such as Dr. Julian Morgenstern claim that both of the holidays (and others, like Kwanzaa) are actually derived from the same pagan holiday celebrating the shortest night of the year. On this night, pagan cultures would "dedicate" temples to their gods by dancing around a fire. It sounds eerie. Especially since the Hebrew word for "dedication" is Chanukah.

Rabbi Ami Silver responds to Julian Morgenstern by saying that he is partially right—but also very wrong. He explains beautifully how the holiday of Chanukah is based on an earlier holiday, but one from the time of Adam HaRishon.

Rabbi Silver starts by pointing out the sources for Chanukah in the Gemara. There are two places it is mentioned. The first is in the section of *Shabbos*, which makes sense. And the second, hinting at what we said above, is in the section of *Avodah Zarah*, idol worship.

In *Shabbos* 22a, the Gemara starts by asking, what is Chanukah? It goes on to describe it as a festival of eight days in which one may not mourn or perform any eulogies. This is really odd, as the first thing that comes to mind for most of us when describing Chanukah is candles, oil, or winning a war. Definitely not some technicality about what we're not allowed to do. Why do the Rabbis in the Gemara describe Chanukah in this way? It gets stranger.

In *Avodah Zarah* 8a, the Rabbis again discuss Chanukah, but this time they are warning the Jews. The Rabbis explain that other religions celebrate similar holidays, and we should make sure not to get confused. Rav Chanan bar Rava tells us about the holiday of Kalenda, which took place for eight days after the winter solstice, and the holiday Saturnura, which took place for eight days before the winter solstice. He is warning us not to confuse these holidays with Chanukah.

These two sections in the Gemara are confusing and raise a lot of questions. However, the next paragraph explains it all.

A *Beraisa* tells a story about Adam. After Adam was kicked out of the Garden of Eden, he was busy living his life, adapting to his circumstances. As time went on, Adam realized something worrisome. The world seemed to be dying! It was getting colder and colder, the sun was getting farther and farther away, and the leaves were falling off the trees. A cold wind was blowing and snow started to fall and Adam assumed the world was returning to its original chaotic state. He started to mourn and cry, thinking this was the death God spoke about when he was banished from the garden. Adam sat on the ground, and for eight days he fasted and cried, eulogizing the world.

Then, on the eighth day something happened. The day was a little bit longer than the day before. The sun was a little bit closer. Adam looked up and realized—this was the natural way of the world! No one was dying and God was not destroying the world; it was merely the changing of the seasons. He then rejoiced for eight days. The next year, when the winter solstice came around, Adam celebrated for all sixteen days as a celebration to God. This holiday was celebrated by all humans for the first few hundred years, and those are the pagan holidays discussed by Dr. Morgenstern and the Gemara.

This could explain why we are not allowed to eulogize or fast on Chanukah, because Adam stopped eulogizing when he realized what was happening. It can also explain why the pagan holidays were so similar: they were copying Adam's holiday, only they were worshipping idols instead. However, it still does not explain what the Maccabees and the oil have to do with Chanukah and how they fit in here.

The story of the *Menorah* echoes the story of the first winter. Just like darkness was turned to light, the candles stayed lit for eight days and the influence of the Greeks was abolished. However, it goes even deeper than that. So deep that we celebrate the oil as the main event, not Adam.

Adam's fear was that he had sinned, and now God was returning the world to chaos and emptiness. He was afraid that God was abandoning him, and then God wasn't—so he celebrated. Fundamentally, Adam had nothing to do with the whole cycle. He was not the reason it started getting warmer; it was the order of nature that God had set up. Adam celebrated because his fear was calmed.

However, that fear would resurface. Not the fear that the world would end, as God promised us after the Flood that it wouldn't. However, the fear that God would abandon us, as the Jewish People, can and did resurface. The same chaos that Adam experienced was experienced by the Jews. Their land was under Greek rule, they were not allowed to study Torah, and idols were everywhere. Worst of all, the Greek culture had permeated so much that it was hard to tell who the enemy was. The Jews were scared, and they wondered: Is this the end of us? Are we going to disappear?

The Maccabees knew the answer. In the case of Adam, he had nothing to do with the world going dark, so he had nothing to do with the world becoming light. However, here the Jews had everything to do with the confusion. They had sinned, and that had led them to where they were in all the chaos. Therefore, the Maccabees stood up and said, "We had a part in making it dark; we need to have a part in making it light." They initiated the fire and then, once God saw that the Jews wanted to be His nation, He took over and did the rest. We lit the *Menorah*, and God made it burn for eight days.

We cannot end the world. God is responsible for nature and how it runs. However, in history and with humanity, the actions of man count. We can make changes and influence God's presence in our world. When we step forward, so does He; when we step back, He does as well.

Chanukah is celebrated close to the winter solstice because it is a time of change, of flipping our trajectory. It is when the days start getting longer and the earth gets warmer. It is the time in which things started looking up for the Jewish nation when they were so scared. For me, Chanukah is a time of changing the script. My son was born on Chanukah, my book was started on Chanukah, and the manuscript was completed and given in to be edited on Chanukah. And the best part is, we only need to find one tiny little jar of oil, and God will do the rest. We only need to turn the wheel a little bit and the whole destination changes.

Take advantage of this time of year, when the dark turns to light. Change something you always wanted to change; flip your trajectory. It's an amazing time to take that one small step.

ASARAH B'TEVES

The tenth day of Teves is a sad day for the Jewish People. We know it is a fast day, and it commemorates the destruction of the Temple, but what exactly happened on this day that was so dreadful, it deserves its own fast day? We learn in *Navi* that on this day, Asarah B'Teves, the Babylonians came and laid siege to the city of Jerusalem.

Yirmiyahu and Yechezkel both discuss the siege. In *Melachim II*, Elisha HaNavi also talks about the siege, however this particular version describes it in a unique way. The prophet talks about how on this day, he received a prophecy from God telling him to write down the exact date, using the words: *"Etzem ha'yom ha'zeh*—This exact day."

What is so special about this phrase?

This is the wording mentioned in the Torah whenever there is a major transition in the world that will changes its status forever. For example, the Torah uses this phrase when Noach and his family board the ark before the Flood. After that day, the world would never be the same again. This phrase is also used when the Jews leave Egypt, showing that something fundamental was shifting, and nothing would ever be the same, for better or for worse.

So, the Babylonians laying siege to Jerusalem is clearly a fundamental, world-changing event. But why?

Let us first understand what a siege is. It is not merely an act of intimidation, to terrify the citizens of the city into surrender. Laying a siege is actually closing off the city's resources. Without the ability to go in or out, there is no economy, no access to food supplies, and few water sources. Within a few weeks, the city experiences famine and starvation.

When the Babylonians laid siege to Jerusalem, they cut off all her resources. They caused starvation and suffering. Many died, and many were killed in the hunt for food. By the time the Babylonians broke in, two years after they laid siege, the residents of the city were so weak and few that they could not defend themselves. Unsurprisingly, they lost the war.

A few months later, on Tzom Gedaliah, Tzidkiyahu was appointed the leader of the Jews that remained in Israel. However, he was murdered by fellow Jews soon after. The Jewish nation lost their home.

We can see clearly now that the siege was the first in a chain of terrible events. It was the beginning of the end, and after the siege was laid, nothing would ever be the same again.

I would say that this day was transformative. It was the moment it became real to the Jews—that they might be in big trouble. Something that seemed impossible became possible.

We fast years later for a simple reason: All throughout history, the impossible happens, and it should serve as a wake-up call for us. While the Jews of Jerusalem, unfortunately, did not wake up, let us do better. Let us learn from their mistakes and take the impossible as a wake-up call.

## TU B'SHEVAT

Tu B'Shevat is the holiday on which we celebrate the birthday of the trees. But when you think about it, it doesn't seem to make a lot of sense: Are all trees born on the same day? No. Was this the day the first tree was created? No.

So why is this a birthday for trees? Imagine we all celebrated our birthdays on one communal day of the year. We would feel utterly nameless. So why are we doing this for the trees? If it's because they are not unique, then why celebrate a birthday for them at all?

Actually, if you look at the origins of Tu B'Shevat, it doesn't seem to be a holiday at all. It was actually tax day.[5] If so, why are we celebrating it?

The Talmud offers an explanation:

The typical rainy season in Israel ends at the beginning of Shevat. By the fifteenth of the month, the trees technically have everything they need to bear fruit. Once the trees have everything they need, we pay taxes, i.e., *korbanos* to God.

However, this sounds almost like celebrating the day you were conceived instead of the day you were born. And paying for it.

What are we actually doing here? When we give a *korban* to our Creator, we are thanking Him. Sending a *korban* from the fruits of the trees is a way of saying thank you that the trees are growing. But the question remains: Why are we bringing a *korban* before the fruit comes out, if it is only potential at this point?

The reason is that we are showing our understanding that we are not in control; God is. By saying thank you before it even happens, we are acknowledging that the outcome is completely up to our Creator. Not only that, but we completely trust Him that He will do what's best for us—so much so that we are thanking Him before He even does it.

We are not celebrating the fruit, and we are not celebrating the tree. We are celebrating our faith in God and His kindness toward us. We are celebrating the relationship.

As a side note, when I spoke about this with others, a common objection came up. How can I say that I fully trust the Creator will do what's best for me, so much so that I thank Him in advance? How can I say this with so much confidence?

It goes back to the story I told at the beginning of the book. I have a deep-rooted faith that whatever happens to me is the best that can

---

5    *Rosh Hashanah* 14a.

happen. I truly and honestly believe that nothing that happened to me was bad for me. It might feel bad, seem bad, and be experienced in a bad way. But there is not one thing in this world that happens out of coincidence, out of spite, or out of punishment. God is Good, and God is God: Every little thing that happens to me in my life is there to help me in some way. And I truly believe that the Master of the entire universe loves me. Can you believe that? He loves *me*! And *you*! This amazing, all-capable God loves me and you!

I know this because when I was in that hospital bed, falling into an abyss, knowing I was going to die, I felt it. I felt His presence, His complete acceptance and love for me, and I wanted nothing more than to lean on it. I woke up and remembered that feeling of security. So today, when a loved one passes away from a terrible illness plaguing the world, or when so many die in soulless terror attacks, I remember that security. I admit that I do not understand it. I admit that I pray that God finds an easier way. But I know, in my heart of hearts, that even if I hate it, it is for our good. Because He loves us.

So, say thank you.

## PURIM

This holiday always bothered me, and once I had kids, to be completely honest, I absolutely dreaded it. It felt like one long, horrible day where I had to take the kids out on the town in their costumes, deal with all the sugar highs, the bathroom breaks, and the inevitable tears (my daughter couldn't eat half the treats because of her allergy). Then we would end up at some party where my husband would have a thoroughly amazing time, and I would be watching cranky, overtired, over-sugared kids in dirty costumes. Then I would drag my drunk husband home and it was all a big joke because that is Purim. I felt like it was definitely not a woman's holiday, if a holiday at all. I simply didn't connect. So, I set about fixing that. What is the real meaning behind Purim? Is it really just about getting drunk and eating sugar?

I found out, in fact, that the whole day is a celebration of a woman's power.

The Rabbis in the Gemara point out that everything in the world is hinted to in the Torah in some way. So where is Haman in the Torah? They answer with the *pasuk*, "*Ha'min ha'eitz ha'zeh*—Did you eat from this tree."[6] *Ha'min* in Hebrew is spelled the same as Haman, and this is where we find Haman in the Torah.

Okay, but why there? What does the tree in the Garden of Eden have to do with the Purim story that occurred thousands of years later?

We spoke above, in the section on good versus evil, about obvious good and inherent good.[7] We spoke about how although chocolate seems good, broccoli is actually better, and how there are two different kinds of good. Also, we mentioned previously that the festivals help us bring the thoughts and lessons into action and into our lives through the yearly calendar.

Here's how the different kinds of good connect to our lives on Purim.

The tree of knowledge gave human beings the ability to choose their moral values. Before Adam and Chavah ate from the tree, there were clear morals that were good and bad, and these were not questioned. Once they ate from the tree, those morals became up for debate. Things weren't clear anymore.

However, human beings also have desires. Therefore, although we technically have the knowledge to dictate morals since we ate from the tree, those morals are skewed because they are led by desires rather than actual differentiation between good and bad.

To make it clearer, imagine someone who is writing out nutrition plans based on what he studied. This person has the knowledge needed to create the nutrition plans. Now let's say we give that person chocolate and broccoli. Here are two elements of good: the nutritional value and the flavor. From a nutrition standpoint, it's easy to say that broccoli is superior, even if they may be tempted to eat the chocolate. When it comes to morals, that temptation is often too hard to bear.

When we are in charge of moral decisions, as opposed to God, those morals become skewed. They are led by the desire for what tastes good, not what is inherently good.

---

6    *Bereishis* 3:11.
7    See chapter 3, "The Torah."

Let's use a drastic example. If you asked Hitler, he probably thought he was doing the world a favor. He did not think of himself as evil, but as someone who was trying to purify the world for the sake of humanity. However, the opposite was true: he was evil incarnate. This is because his morals became skewed when he let his human desires dictate them.

What does any of this have to do with Purim?

There are a lot of parallels that can be drawn:

- Haman had everything, but he wasn't happy because he couldn't have Mordechai's respect. In the same token, Adam had all the trees, but was not happy since he could not have one particular tree.

- Haman's wife and Adam's wife both had a negative influence on their husbands. Zeresh told Haman to get a tree and build gallows, and Chavah told Adam to eat from the fruit on the tree. That tree ultimately became Haman's death trap, and the tree Adam eats—makes him mortal and brings death to the world.

- The example that really gets me is how Haman wanted to pretend to be a king—and said as much when he was asked what the reward should be for the man the king wishes to honor. Flip to the Eden story, and Adam ate from the tree and started to dictate morals, pretending he was God!

The parallels do not end there. The couples have parallels as well. Achashveirosh and Esther versus Adam and Chavah.

- Achashveirosh looks for a mate in all the girls in his kingdom, as does Adam who looks for a mate in all the animals.

- God made a miracle and Esther was chosen, just like He created Chavah and made Adam's match. He chose, in a revealing way, both matches.

- Esther is told to keep her identity secret and keep this knowledge hidden, and Chavah is told to abstain from the Tree of Knowledge.

- The Creator "walks" around the garden as Mordechai walks around the palace gates.

- Esther is commanded by Mordechai to reveal her identity and gives the knowledge over, while Chavah forces Adam to eat the fruit and reveals the knowledge to him.

I know, this is heavy and technical, but bear with me because I'm presenting my point.

What is the connection between Chavah and Esther? They were both put in shockingly similar situations where they have significant control and influence over their husbands:

- Chavah did not use this power well and humanity suffered.
- Esther realizes that she is being given the opportunity to fix the sin—or at least a part of it.

She tells Mordechai to command the Jews to fast, which is the opposite of what they did in the Garden of Eden. She then takes it upon herself to rectify the sin. In other words, Chavah used food to mix up morals and dictate them based on desire, so Esther uses food to teach Achashveirosh the difference between what we desire and what is right.

At the feast, Esther tells Achashveirosh: If you desire me, come again for another feast. She is showcasing his desires. Then, at the second feast, she tells him she is asking for her life. She is presenting him with a moral choice, the opportunity to choose good. But then she makes it hard. She points to Haman and says "He is evil"—although he "tastes" good to you, he is morally wrong. Get rid of him. Achashveirosh listens and she succeeds in rectifying a small part of Chavah's sin: correcting the wrong.

But she doesn't stop there. She asks Achashveirosh to show what he has learned, perhaps to show God that she, as a woman, had been in the same situation as Chavah—with the same power of influence—and she had used it correctly.

Esther asks Achashveirosh to rip up the decree. This is a tough request: he has no personal need to do so, as his own beloved wife will be safe regardless of what happens to her people. Furthermore, such a move would look bad for him politically—but he does it anyway. He chooses moral good over what he desires. Esther has managed to influence the king for good.

On a side note, Zeresh (majorly!) failed here. She chose to harp on Haman's weakness, his ego, and tried to influence him to be bigger. When he came home complaining about Mordechai, she negatively influenced her husband and pushed him to kill Mordechai. Rabbi David Fohrman takes it a step further and points out that Esther asked Achashveirosh to love her for who she was, even though she was a Jewess, while Zeresh asked Haman to change, making him think he was not good enough.

When you get into it, the whole Purim story is about one woman who took it upon herself to fix Chavah's sin. She was greatly rewarded, and her son was the one who rebuilt the Beis Hamikdash. Purim is about the women and their power of influence on the world and people around them. It is about using that power to fix the sin, and to help others make the right decisions.

We see that a superficial cultural understanding of our tradition can lead to resentment. Deeper understanding leads to connection and joy. How to practically connect to this holiday, I do not yet know. But it is nice to know what it stands for and go from there.

## PESACH

What is Pesach even about?

I know, it's about removing all the chametz, and we were always taught that the chametz is a symbol for the sin in our life. However, I really never connected to that. Isn't that Yom Kippur? I have always had a hard time connecting to this holiday. I mean I get it—we became God's nation—but we celebrate that every single day, we pray and keep Shabbos, and we dress like royalty.

I reached out to Manya Lazaroff, one of my mentors, to see if she had any insight that would help me connect to the holiday more, and not just see it as an awesome vacation or a slave drive. She had the most amazing answer.

When Hashem took the Jews out of Mitzrayim, He literally had to take them out. They didn't want to leave! Can you imagine being a slave stuck in horrible, useless labor and being beaten almost to death? Being starved, and having your children yanked from you—and yet, when someone offers you freedom, you say no? No, I'll just stay here and suffer, thank you.

Sounds crazy, but that is exactly what happened. The Jews were stuck in such a victim and slave mentality that they couldn't believe it was even possible for them to leave. It made no sense to them, and the unknown was terrifying. They opted for the known, and what they were used to—terrible as it was. The Creator would not stand for that, though, and He literally scooped them out.

Now, thousands of years later, what is our focus? What are we working on or enhancing within ourselves during this holiday? We are not in Egypt, and we are not enslaved. How do we connect to this holiday and how it relates to us? By getting out of our own suffering and removing the victimhood, the slavery, and the mentality of "oh, it just isn't possible; it's easier to stay put."

As a personal example (because why not when you already know all the personal details about me), I also thought I was stuck in a trap that was impossible to get out of. I suffer from misophonia, a phobia of sounds. It is a form of anxiety where certain specific sounds send you very quickly and very suddenly into a full-blown panic attack. I'll be honest: it sucks. However, I never really did anything about it.

Why? Because misophonia is not something you are born with. One hundred percent of the time it stems from trauma. And I was not interested in learning which trauma it was, reliving it, and dealing with all of that. It was easier to just avoid those specific sounds as much as possible and have the occasional, very real panic attack.

However, thankfully, the people around me were not "down for that." During the coronavirus lockdown, when I couldn't really avoid much of anything around me, it got too much to bear, and I went to therapy. Now, keep in mind that I already knew my therapist and felt incredibly safe with her. However, I still fought her. I still didn't want to believe that the condition was fixable…Because that would require me fixing it.

But we did it. We identified what I am afraid might happen when I hear those sounds, we identified why I felt like it might happen, and we came up with coping skills for me to remind myself that it will not happen. When I felt safe enough, we even explored the memories a bit and tried to reprocess them so that a future attack would be smaller...and it worked.

The crazy thing is that I can't believe I let myself be so limited for so many years! What was I thinking? I literally failed tests in school because someone was chewing gum—all because I wasn't brave enough to get myself out of the slavery.

Don't be me.

Don't wait twenty-five years to figure it out.

Take this Pesach and get out of your slavery; believe there is something better out there and that it's worth the desert you have to travel through. Believe that the Creator has your back, and that anything is possible. Get yourself out of the victim mentality.

How, you may ask?

Well, with the Haggadah, of course.

Every step in the *Seder* is another opportunity for us to open our minds to the possibilities before us. Want to see?

- *Kadesh* and *Urchatz*: Taking a moment to set aside the time for this special mitzvah and to purify ourselves.
- *Karpas*: Dipping the raw vegetable—which reminds us of hard, useless labor—into salt water. Sending us the message that all those stresses and limits we put on ourselves, all those temporary problems we agonize over, are useless and will only end in tears. We need to prioritize, see what is really important and useful, and work on that.
- *Yachatz*: We break the matzah and put the bigger part away for later. Why? To teach us that the big things are worth waiting for; that focusing on the small things and doing them correctly will lead to the ultimate big-ticket item. It's all about being able to see the full picture and the long-term goal. Not getting stuck in excuses and the now.
- *Maggid*: Tell the story. Communicate. Talk to the next generation, talk to the people you need to talk to. Communication is key to overcoming any obstacle, even if that means communicating with yourself or talking to a therapist. Talk about it and tell your story; it will make the load easier to bear.

- *Rachtzah*: We wash our hands before we eat. Why? To remind us to elevate even the simplest of things—not to get stuck in the mundane and stay low but to take everything we are doing and make it special, high, and directed toward the ultimate goal, whatever that may be. Don't look down; look ahead and up, and elevate what you are doing. Always remember that even the most menial and mundane task can be special if you make it so.

- *Motzi Matzah*: We eat a sandwich made out of unleavened bread. This flat bread represents humility, not being full of ourselves (with yeast). Sometimes, we are so sure we know there is no solution, so certain that nothing can help us. Take a step down, accept help, accept that there might be a better way. And take it—because it will help you. Let your Creator lead you there and help you.

- *Maror*: Recognizing the bitter. It is so, so important to understand and acknowledge that there is an issue in order to be able to overcome the problem. So many times, I have seen people complain about things and then claim there is nothing wrong with them: the whole wide world is the issue, not them. I have seen people complain about a medical ailment but refuse to go to a doctor because, why should they? They're fine, and doctors just cause pain. No, we need to acknowledge that "hey, there's a problem here"; I feel sick, I feel sad, I feel stressed. Let's figure out what the problem is, feel it, and validate it so we can move on from it.

- *Korech*: We eat a sandwich consisting of matzah, humbleness; maror, bitterness; and charoses, sweetness. We eat this to understand that the world is complex. It is possible to feel more than one thing at any one time. Feelings, experiences, and emotions can all have mixed effects. Yes, the Jewish nation has had a hard history, but we also have an amazing identity, and the Creator of the world on our side—which is why we've had a challenging history: people are jealous. It is all intertwined, and it is a sign of maturity and growth when we can hold all this in one hand, and take one bite of it all.

- *Shulchan Orech*: Lets eat! Being religious, a follower of the Creator, and a spiritually oriented person doesn't mean we shouldn't enjoy life! No, on the contrary, enjoy every minute and make use of every minute! Enjoy the gifts He gave you! Eat!
- *Tzafun*: Finding that special matzah, the big one we put away for later. Now that we've done all the necessary work, we are able to uncover our potential and achieve that big goal. We've thought long term, we've accomplished the goals on the way, and now we can enjoy the fruits of our labor by being the person we have strived to become. We found our potential.
- *Barech*: Say thank you. Yes, we have come this far, but also say thank you on the way. Appreciation is a gift to the person giving us something, but it is also a gift to ourselves. It is being able to recognize the good, see the positive for what it is, and to communicate and express that. Appreciation does wonders to our soul. Be grateful for what you have; it will bring you more.
- *Hallel*: Go all out. It is not enough to just say thank you. Let us truly be happy for what we have in this world. For a moment, let us put aside our sorrows and stresses and let's dance! Let's sing about all the good things we have. Let's sing to the One who gave them to us. Let's be happy!
- *Nirtzah*: Next year in a (peaceful) Jerusalem. Jerusalem will only be at peace when the world is perfected and reached its ultimate goal. Let us pray that if we didn't yet get there this year, then next year we certainly will.

And in case you needed a little extra push to leave Mitzrayim. In English, the translation of Mitzrayim is "constraints." Do the Seder, work through the steps, and get out of your constraints! Become the person you always knew you could be!

I love Pesach.

## LAG BA'OMER

Lag Ba'omer is a special day, especially in Israel. It is a day where we go out, make bonfires, and sing all night. It is a night of togetherness when all Jewish souls just unite. But why? What is so special about this day?

As we know, it is the day that Rabbi Shimon Bar Yochai passed away. However, "yahrzeits" are usually not celebrated in this way. What is going on here?

Maybe we should start by talking about who Rabbi Shimon Bar Yochai ("Rashbi" for short) was.

In the Gemara in *Maseches Shabbos*, there is a story about him. The Rabbis tell us that the Romans heard that Rabbi Shimon had criticized them and said bad things about their roads and cities. They had sentenced him to death, and he and his son were on the run for their lives. They hid in a cave for twelve years where they were sustained by a spring and a carob tree that miraculously grew near the cave.

When they came out of the cave after twelve years of learning in solitude, they saw people sowing seeds in their fields. Rashbi took one look at them and criticized them for focusing on their fields when there was so much spirituality and Torah to focus on. He was so enraged he literally lit them on fire with his eyes, and kept lighting fires everywhere he looked.

A Voice from Heaven cried out and asked, "Did you come to destroy My world? Go back into your cave!"

So Rashbi and his son went back into their cave for another year and learned a bit more—this time about this world, the people in it, and how they are holy as well. They emerged from the cave as the year ended, and this time their reaction was a little different. Rabbi Shimon Bar Yochai's son continued burning everything with his eyes, while Rabbi Shimon would fix all that he destroyed.

What is going on here? What's with the superpower of sending fire from the eyes? It seems to be a bit of an "out there" story, but even if it were normal, what had changed for Rabbi Shimon over the course of the year that enabled him to heal everything his son burned?

After repairing the damage done by his son, Rashbi looked at him and said, "We are enough for this world." However, this only adds to the confusion. What is going on here? Reading this story instills more fear than a desire to dance around a bonfire.

A story that occurred a while after they emerged from the cave may help explain this.

One Friday afternoon, as Shabbos was approaching, Rabbi Shimon and his son saw an old man walking down the road. He was holding big bundles of myrtle branches and running. The duo stopped him and asked him why he was holding the myrtle branches, and he responded, "For Shabbos!" Asked Rashbi, "Is one not enough?" The old man responded, "No, one is for *zachor* and one is for *shamor*." Rashbi heard this, looked at his son, and said, "See how much the Jewish People love the mitzvos!" After this, they both relaxed and nothing more was destroyed through them.

The questions still remain, but let's look at the evolution of Rashbi's vision for a moment:

- When he first comes out of the cave, it is with burning eyes.
- The second time he emerges, they are healing eyes—repairing all that his son destroys.
- Finally, when he meets the man holding his Shabbos flowers, his eyes are at ease.

We can understand what Rashbi went through if we consider what it must have been like in the cave. No distractions, no worry about food or drink, and every waking moment spent in holiness. In the cave, Rashbi and his son lived in a dimension completely above the physical world—both because their needs were met and because of their Torah study—that could not even see the importance of the physical world. However, while this may be amazing in the spiritual world, thinking in such black-and-white terms is not sustainable once you are out of your bubble, or your cave. Therefore, when they emerged from the cave the first time, thinking only in black-and-white, purely spiritual terms, they saw everything as either good or evil—and all physical tasks were evil by virtue of them not being spiritual. Therefore, they destroyed them.

Take it a step further: When Rashbi judged the world harshly, with no leniency, and no understanding, he destroyed the world. Whether we understand this as literal or metaphorical, judging harshly—in black-and-white terms—destroys the world. What is interesting is that the Creator did not like this. He said, "Did you come to destroy my world? Who asked you to judge My creations so harshly? Go back to your cave!"

To the Creator, it did not matter how spiritually high Rashbi and his son were, if they were going to judge people harshly, they could go back into hiding!

A year later, the Creator tells Rashbi to try again. This time, he comes out, and without changing an ounce of his values, he judges everyone favorably. How?

The answer lies in the sentence Rashbi said to his son after the second time: "We are enough for the world." Yes, the rest of the world might be doing something you deem wrong. Maybe you are right, and they are wasting their time. But that is not for us to decide, or to act on. Our doing the right thing is enough for the world to stand. When each person worries about their own mitzvos, their own soul, the world can stand. Care for your fellow human as a human, but don't judge and worry so much whether they are doing the right thing or not.

This is beautiful, but there is still something missing here, right? Rashbi and his son come out of the cave, judged everyone harshly, and destroyed the world—literally or metaphorically. They went back into the cave and came out again, this time calmer. They told themselves that yes, everyone might be doing the wrong thing, but that's okay.

There is still something wrong here. They are still judging harshly. Yes, it is less destructive, but it's still not the ideal.

This is where the old man running with his myrtle branches comes in. Rashbi decides not to immediately judge him and instead has a conversation with him. In doing so, he realizes how special and holy this simple Jew is. He is filled with wonder and looks at his son, exclaiming, "How special are the Jewish People, who love the mitzvos so much!"

Now, not only is he not destroying—not only is he not judging—he is accepting. He is saying: We are all correct in our own way. We are all different, but we are all holy and special to the Creator.

This is amazing! This is worth dancing around a bonfire for.

We learn from Rashbi and his journey that we can and should accept all Jews—not just despite their flaws—but accept them as intrinsically holy and special Jews, who are beautiful in every way. If we can, we should try to see them with no flaws at all! It is not our place to see and judge others' faults; only to recognize the beauty in differences and just love each other. We need to leave the judging to the Creator and view ourselves as equals in our love for the Creator and His mitzvos.

This is why on the anniversary of Rabbi Shimon Bar Yochai's death, we celebrate the lesson he taught us. We build bonfires, and instead of using them to destroy, we use them to unite the Jewish People. We dance with our fellow Jews who look nothing like us, and we love them whole heartedly because they are special to the Creator.

How incredible is this day?

## SHAVUOS

You know what is interesting about Shavuos? It is not actually on a physical date. All the other holidays are on a specific date in the calendar, but Shavuos is fifty days from Pesach. It's not noted as "on the sixth day of the third month," but as "seven weeks and a day" from the second day of Pesach. Why?

Shavuos is when we celebrate our transformation from a group of people to a nation. It is when we celebrate receiving the Torah and officially becoming the Chosen People. It is also the day we read the story of Rus and Boaz.

The story of Rus has so many interesting aspects. She was a princess of the lowest nation on earth, a nation full of promiscuity and violence. A nation whose name itself describes its lowly origins: Moav, meaning "from father," recalling the fact that it was the result of an incestuous relationship. Yet Rus not only leaves that nation and becomes a Jew—she becomes the grandmother of King David, the king of the Jewish nation. How bizarre! But is it?

The Jewish nation was not always so high and lofty. As a matter of fact, we started off as low as they come. When we were in Egypt, we were on the lowest level of impurity. That means we passed the lowest level of purity, and then went down even further, passing all the levels of impurity. We were very far behind. However, by the time we reached Har Sinai we were on the highest level of purity, we had climbed up and up and reached the top. This is the first part of why we count the days from Pesach until Shavuos. We are marking the journey from the lowest of lows to the highest of highs.

But why fifty specifically?

There is a deeper meaning to the number. We know that in Kabbalah, seven is a holy number. It is the number of completion. There are seven days in a week, seven directions in space, and seven in Hebrew means "completely satisfied." It is the max in this world. Then we have the number eight, seven plus one, which symbolizes otherworldliness. On the eighth day, we perform the *bris milah*, and in Hebrew the number eight means "fat," expressing that it is more than full.

Now, how do we reach the max of the max? Multiply seven by seven and you get forty-nine. And how do you get the otherworldliness? Add one. This is why the Torah is given on day fifty. Once you have gone through all the different levels in this world and you have maxed out, take one more step into the spiritual world, and you get the Torah.

Shavuos is not about the day itself; even its name makes that clear. It is about the weeks leading up to it, the counting, the *sefiras ha'omer*. Make every day count.

## SHIVAH ASAR B'TAMMUZ

As usual, when looking into the meaning of a day in the Jewish calendar, the first thing we look at is what happened on that date (in different years), in this case, the seventeenth of Tammuz.

Here goes:

- The walls of Jerusalem were breached and the fall of the Beis Hamikdash began.
- The constant pillar of smoke that would rise from the *Mizbei'ach*, the altar on which the Kohanim would sacrifice the animals, stopped rising.
- The *Sefer Torah* was taken out of the Beis Hamikdash and burned.
- Idols were placed in the Beis Hamikdash in its stead.
- Much earlier on this date, the Jews built the golden calf.

Now, up until this last point, I was all in. All these terrible things happened that led to the destruction of the Temple, and today we are sad about that. They even all happened on the same date, which shows the significance of the day.

But what does the golden calf have to do with this? To me it didn't seem to have anything to do with the events of the destruction of the Beis Hamikdash.

I decided to find out what exactly happened when the Jews created the golden calf. They asked Aharon to "create a god to walk in front of them."

Rabbi Fohrman brings up a valid question. The Jewish People were missing Moshe. Moshe, their leader, had gone up to the Har Sinai to receive the Torah and had not yet come back down. If they were missing Moshe, why not ask for a new leader? Why did they ask for a new god? It doesn't seem to make sense. When I heard this question, I realized this was not the first time the Jews had tried replacing God. When they received the Ten Commandments, they asked Moshe to speak to God rather than Him speaking directly to them. Even when they spoke about who took them out of Egypt, they said, "Moshe took us out." Not God. It might be a tangent, but why were they being so distant? If we spoke about the ultimate goodness being closeness to the Creator, why are they trying to get away?

Rabbi Fohrman answers with the words used to describe the golden calf in the Torah. The word "*masechah*" is used, meaning a solid piece of material. However, it can also mean "mask." The Jewish People were, plain and simple, scared; they were asking for some kind of barrier: a mask.

Yes, this amazing all-powerful God took them out of Egypt and saved them—but look at how powerful He is! Look what He did to the Egyptians. That could be us next time. They were frightened, and no matter how much Moshe or even God tried to convince them otherwise, they kept using Moshe as a boundary to create distance between themselves and the Creator.

When Moshe did not come back down, and the *eiruv rav* showed them the image of Moshe dead, their fear grew. The safety barrier they had placed between themselves and this all-powerful Creator had been destroyed, and now they were really afraid of God. So, they built their own barrier. A kind of intermediary to protect them from the actual God. Something that would serve as the go-between so they would not have to meet face-to-face with this intimidating Creator.

There is something inherently beautiful in bringing the spirituality into the physical. Bringing a physical memento to something intangible. However, when that physical memento becomes the focus and acts as a distraction or a boundary, there is a loss of the beauty and something ugly comes instead. While from far it may look beautiful, it is a knockoff and empty of value.

That is why Moshe broke the *Luchos*. When he saw the Jewish People using intermediaries and barriers and all different kinds of protection, he knew they would misuse the *Luchos*. Moshe understood that while they were still in that place of fear, they would focus so hard on the *Luchos* that they would forget what they represented. They had become empty of value to the people, and therefore, Moshe broke them.

Interestingly enough, they did not lose their inherent value. My father talked about this when he opened his publishing company. The company is called Mosaica, alluding to a mosaic of the broken *Luchos*. My father explained that it is our job throughout the generations to find those little shattered fragments of the *Luchos*, bring them to light, and fit them back together. In his way, he is doing that by publishing books that bring light from all over. But we can each do this in our way by finding the sparks, the broken pieces, and bringing them back together.

But back to the seventeenth of Tammuz: what does all this have to do with the destruction of the Temple or the other four tragedies that happened on this day?

All five tragedies have a common value in that a symbol was destroyed:

- The *Luchos* were a symbol of our commitment to the Creator and His to us.
- The walls of Jerusalem were a symbol of the Creator's protection of us.
- The smoke was a symbol of our connection.
- The *Sefer Torah* was a symbol of our partnership.
- The Beis Hamikdash was the ultimate symbol of love, the place where we "met."

We used the symbols incorrectly by trying to create borders and distance ourselves. Unfortunately, that is no less relevant today.

We need to take this day to demonstrate that we want closeness, that we are here without any symbols distancing us from the Creator. That we know how to use mementos.

It is a day of destruction from which we can learn how to rebuild. It gives us the opportunity to showcase our desire for connection and pray for it. Which we will do for the next three weeks.

## TISHAH B'AV

I know this is supposed to be the saddest day in the year, but after being sad for three weeks, what exactly is different about this day? And, are we really sad, or just going through the motions every year because we're expected to? How do I make Tishah B'Av actually mean something real to me?

When we read the book of *Eichah*, something always stood out to me. If Tishah B'Av is about the Beis Hamikdash, why are there all these other stories in it? Turns out this day is not just about the Temples burning; those were just the worst on a long list of suffering the Jewish nation has endured. We use this day to mourn the Temples for many reasons.

But can we mourn them? They didn't happen to us. Yes, the Holocaust is close enough to strike a chord, but even then, how much do we feel the exile on a day-to-day basis?

Rebbetzin Lori Palatnik once gave a talk on Tishah B'Av that really affected me. I connected to what she said. She wasn't trying to convince me how my life is so bad right now and we need Mashiach (which we do). Rather, she said, picture the following:

Imagine that you're working really hard on a masterpiece of art. You work on it for months. Finally, it's ready, and you take it to the art gallery to be displayed. However, tragedy strikes; the place burns down and your masterpiece is gone. Imagine that feeling, how sad and broken you would feel. Now imagine it times one hundred.

I loved this idea and here is why.

It is not about feeling the loss right now today. It is about understanding what we have been through as a nation, how much effort has been put it and how much sorrow we have been through. We need the *geulah*. Don't try to apply it today; rather, close your eyes and put yourself in those earlier days. Imagine the Temple burning, imagine people fleeing the Expulsion in Spain, imagine the concentration camps. Then, imagine what it was like before. Imagine Europe before the war. Imagine Spain in the Golden Age. Imagine Yerushalayim in the time of King Solomon. When you envision the difference between before and after, you realize what we are missing—and that's when you can connect and pray for those good times to come again, this time to stay.

It is not always about bringing the tragedy here. Sometimes it is about remembering the tragedy, imagining ourselves there, and praying that will it never happen again. Recreating that masterpiece.

# AFTERWORD

Dear Reader,

Thank you for taking out the time to read this book. I appreciate that you have taken it as seriously as I have, and I hope it has impacted you as much as it has impacted me. It has been about four years from when I wrote the introduction until I am writing this afterword, and so much has changed.

Please reach out on Instagram @questioningtheanswers with any questions or comments or to continue this journey of learning. You can also email me at kaylahaber@gmail.com. I look forward to connecting with you.

We are each on our own journey. Let's try to help each other along our way and leave the judging to God. Here's to acceptance!

May we all merit to read this book and many more in a rebuilt Jerusalem and in peace.

*Kayla*

# QUESTIONS AND ANSWERS WITH ILANA COWLAND

I wanted to give a space for you to hear from one of my mentors. I mention many times in this book the importance of finding your spiritual leaders. I wanted to showcase the value of having guidance, and most importantly, enable you to gain from some of her teachings on topics or ideas this book did not cover.

## ILANA COWLAND

Originally from London, Mrs. Cowland attended Hasmonean High School. After high school, she attended BJJ Seminary in Jerusalem and then received a BA in Jewish Studies from the University of London, as well as a diploma in counseling. Having spent nine years working as a *rebbetzin* in the London Aish HaTorah community, she and her family moved to Jerusalem in 2004 where she has been involved in teaching and education administration, including three years as the principal of a seminary for high school graduates. Mrs. Cowland is a sought-after lecturer and educator internationally, with a specialty in the topics of relationships and women's issues. In addition to teaching seminary students, Mrs. Cowland is involved in teaching *shalom bayis* courses to young married women in Jerusalem. She lives with her family in Ramot Bet and has agreed to answer a few questions for us from her perspective.

*What is the definition of God?*

The Jewish definition of God is the Creator, Sustainer, and Supervisor.

*If God created us to give to us, doesn't that make God inherently selfish?*

There are two questions in this question:

- If we were never created, we would never have known the difference.
- If He needed to give to us, isn't that selfish?

We have to understand that as people, whenever we give, there is a slightly selfish motivation. We, being selfish, assume that everyone is just like us. If we give selfishly, then surely God must do so as well. The reason we give selfishly is that God made us for pleasure, and so we get a selfish pleasure from everything we do. But that's the nature of created beings. If they were created for pleasure, everything gives us pleasure. Even giving. God is not created and is not bound to the same rules of human nature. When God gives, it's real. It's a petty mistake to project our motivations on Him. While it's true that had we not been created, we would never have known the difference, in order to be given pleasure, we obviously needed to have been created.

*What is a good rabbi?*

Someone whose learning has helped him see and weigh up situations "through Heaven's eyes," and to follow on that theme, who is also able to see the worth of the person in front of him. His job is to bridge the gap—honestly and without an axe to grind—between the emotional needs of the human who is asking and the intellectual value system ascribed by the Torah. This way he can help the person asking the question to find their individual answer, with sensitivity to the person's pain and a fair evaluation of what the person is capable of. All delivered with patience and love.

*Why do we pray by graves and not straight to the Creator?*

It's a mistake to pray to a dead person. It happens a lot. It's okay to be inspired by the channels opened up by *tzaddikim* of the past and to use that inspiration to pray to God. But Jews only pray to God.

*Why do we have laws about how to dress as women?*

I could go on all day...but to be brief, women have, among other things, two strong attributes:

- The ability to sense how to make connections with the people around them
- The ability to be in touch with their whole self, their depth, etc.

These two aspects are at odds. I really know who I am as a person, and I really want to connect to you by sensing what makes you happy. So, do I keep my clothes on or take them off? The part of me that wants to be treated as a person and related to like a woman—not just as a body or a piece of meat—is telling me to stay dressed. Yet, the part of me that wants to connect to the world and please the world—and senses how much the world appreciates the physical body of the woman—wants to share my body with the world. Just look at the media: half the time, women are in suits trying to be taken seriously, and half the time, they're half naked! (When was the last time you saw a half-naked man at the Oscars? That's right, never.)

It's confusing to be a woman. So Judaism relieves us of this conflict. It sets the guidelines for us, and this makes it easier for us not to make the mistakes that can really hurt us. First and foremost, you are a woman, a person, a mind, a being, a soul. Make sure you dress that way to the public so that they never mistake you for or treat you as an object, a body, a piece of meat, a slave, or a subordinate. And then, in relationships with other women or with family or in marriage, where you do not risk being treated as nothing more than a body, the laws of dress relax.

I have a body, true.

I am a body, false.

*Why are the more religious groups against feminism?*

The original feminist agenda was to share the male platform of success. Western success is based on money, wealth, status, career, etc. In order for women to share the accolade of success, they needed to share the money, wealth, and status platform. To the extent that women were not given these equal opportunities, they were being deprived of the opportunity for success.

You'll notice that these are not great definitions of success. (You can be miserable and corrupt. But as long as you're wealthy, you're a success. Congratulations.) They are also not very Jewish ones. We value things like impact, contribution, fulfillment, education, family, mission, legacy, ethics, happiness, and God-consciousness.

In a world whose definition of success was male and therefore where only men were successful, feminism had to fight for equality.

In a system whose definition of success is not particular to men, equality is not necessary. If anything, it's insulting. Why do I, a fabulous, functional woman, need to be like a man in order to be considered a success? It's as insulting as telling a man he has to be like a woman to be valuable! The feminist fight is not a Jewish one. In the Jewish platform, all humans have the opportunity for success based on our definitions.

*Why do men wear a kippah?*

I think it's to be seen as a prop to help them with their constant obligation of God consciousness. It's a metaphor for "there is a constant presence above me." (Women sense this instinctively, and therefore don't need the prop.)

*Why are the laws of niddah so strict and extensive, and why all the extra laws?*

Ah! This is the relationship we're supposed to enjoy the most! Every boundary creates a new sensitivity. If actual intimacy was the only thing prohibited during *niddah*, then that is what we would crave. If we were only forbidden from kissing, then that's what we would crave. But look how clever the Torah is! Every single thinkable physical interaction is off the table. So suddenly, we crave it all! How else would holding hands after forty years of marriage still be exciting other than by making it off bounds for half the month? It's an exhaustive, annoying, and ingenious set of laws that allow us to appreciate every single physical interaction when we're allowed it!

## Is physical intimacy before marriage a sin?

Sure. But apart from being a sin (I hate that word...it's so Christian!), it's a terrible shame. I know that not doing so seems archaic, but the following is still true of people today: When people are not completely committed to each other, they take what they can from a relationship. When people are completely committed, they give what they can.

The best kind of intimate experience is when everyone feels safe—not worried about whether the other person will still want to be with them the next day, and when it's okay to be vulnerable. The most guaranteed way to do that is to ensure a total sense of commitment. We Jews call that marriage.

## Why is Judaism so obsessed with time?

Because time is life's measurement, and life is precious.

## What is the Jewish view on mental illness?

Most human beings are judged on their choices. In order to be involved in the spiritual side of life, you have to be in a space wherein you can make choices. Mental illness precludes that. Therefore, mental health is a necessary prerequisite for spiritual growth. When spiritual growth has been prioritized over mental health, we can also assume that spiritual growth has been misunderstood as purely behavioral and not choice based. We must, if we want to grow, take our mental health extremely seriously. (If you're asking about people with special needs who can never make choices or recover, that's a whole different answer based on *tikkun* and *gilgul*.)

## Why is Judaism taught more through fear and less through love?

Fear was the normal way to serve God in the previous generations. We have changed and therefore the newer, acceptable way to relate to God in our generation is primarily through love. Some educational systems are still catching up. Very traditional institutions take a while to trust change. Be patient. We're getting there.

# Bibliography

Aron, Raphael. *Spirituality & Intimacy*. Mosaica Press, 2016.

Ben Maimon, Moshe. *Mishneh Torah, Sefer Mada*, n.d.

Fine, Rabbi Daniel. "Introduction to Sefer Tehillim." sacps.org.uk. https://www.sacps.org.uk/Virtual/Introduction%20to%20Sefer%20 Tehillim.pdf.

"Heart Beat." Cleveland Clinic, 2019. https://my.clevelandclinic.org/ health/articles/17064-heart-beat#:~:text=Your%20heartbeat%20 is%20triggered%20by,atrium%2C%20called%20the%20SA%20node.

Jacobson, Simon. "Women & Men." Chabad.Org. Accessed January 12, 2021. https://www.chabad.org/therebbe/article_cdo/aid/60694/ jewish/Women-Men.htm.

Kaplan, Aryeh, and Abraham Sutton. *Innerspace*. Reprint, Jerusalem: Moznaim, 1990.

Kluger, Rabbi Avrohom Tzvi. *My Sole Desire*. Reprint, Feldheim, 2021.

Kook, Avraham Yitzchak HaCohen. *Olat Reiyah*, n.d.

Kosman, Miriam. *Circle, Arrow, Spiral: Exploring Gender in Judaism*. Menucha Publishers, 2014.

Kurzweil, Andrew. "Rabbi Adin Steinsaltz: 'From the Day of Birth to the Last Breath.'" Arthur Kurzweil, 2019. https://arthurkurzweil.com/2019/03/ rabbi-adin-steinsaltz-from-the-day-of-birth-to-the-last-breath/.

Morgenstern, Julian. "The Chanukkah Festival and the Calendar of Ancient Israel," *Hebrew Union College Annual*, vol. 20 (1947): 1–136. JSTOR. Accessed April 21, 2021.

"Nothing Comes from Nothing." Parmenides, 2020. http://parmenides.
me/nothing-comes-from-nothing/&sa=D&ust=1608803508737000
&usg=AOvVaw35wLSfML9RWLclfeCbKeCF.

Ramban. *Commentary on the Torah, Shemos* 13:17.

Sacks, Rabbi Lord Jonathan. "Bereishis (5772) – The Faith of God."
Blog. *Covenant & Conversation*, 2011. https://rabbisacks.org/
covenant-conversation-5772-Bereishis-the-faith-of-god/.

Sapirman, Rabbi Dovid. *Emunah: A Refresher Course.* Reprint, Mosaica
Press, 2015.

Simon, Rabbi Levi. "Divine Providence." Dayton Jewish
Observer, 2013. https://daytonjewishobserver.org/2013/07/
divine-providence/.

Spiro, Ken. *Crash Course in Jewish History.* Reprint, Targum
Press, 2001.

The Gutnick Edition Chumash, 2003.

Tilles, Yerachmiel. "What Is Kabbalah? And Why?" Chabad.org, 2021.
https://www.chabad.org/Kabbalah/article_cdo/aid/380664/jewish/
What-is-Kabbalah-And-Why.htm.

# ABOUT THE AUTHOR

Kayla Goldstein is an interior designer living in New York with her husband and two kids. Born in Australia to a leading rabbi and *rebbetzin*, raised in Israel, and currently living in the United States, Kayla has seen a wide spectrum of different approaches to Judaism. Today, running her organization, Questioning the Answers, Kayla seeks to build up the women of Klal Yisrael and empower them to own their Judaism and be proud and fulfilled. Reach out to her on Instagram @questioningtheanswers for bookings or just to have a conversation.

# NOTES

_____

_____

_____

_____

_____

_____

_____

_____

_____

_____

_____

_____

_____

_____

_____

_____

_____

_____

_____

_____

_____

_____

_____

_____

## MOSAICA PRESS

### BOOK PUBLISHERS

*Elegant, Meaningful & Bold*

info@MosaicaPress.com
www.MosaicaPress.com

The Mosaica Press team of
acclaimed editors and designers
is attracting some of the most
compelling thinkers and teachers
in the Jewish community today.
Our books are available around
the world.

HARAV YAACOV HABER
RABBI DORON KORNBLUTH